JEWELRY ARTS WORKSHOP

MW01012015

Pure Silver
Metal
Clay
Beads

**Creative Publishing
international**

First published in the United States of America by
Creative Publishing international, Inc., a member of
Quayside Publishing Group
400 First Avenue North, Suite 300
Minneapolis, MN 55401
1-800-328-3895
www.creativepub.com

ISBN-13: 978-1-58923-611-0
ISBN-10: 1-58923-611-4

10 9 8 7 6 5 4 3 2 1

Library of Congress Cataloging-in-Publication Data
Kaye-Moses, Linda.
    Jewelry arts workshop : pure silver metal clay beads / Linda Kaye-Moses.
        p. cm.
    Includes index.
    ISBN-13: 978-1-58923-443-7
    ISBN-10: 1-58923-443-X
    1. Jewelry making. 2. Silverwork. 3. Beads. I. Title.
    TT212.K39 2009
    739.27--dc22
                                        2008052415

Technical Editor: Tamara L. Honaman
Copy Editor: India R. Tresselt
Proofreader: Karen Ruth
Book Design and Page Layout: Laura H. Couallier, Laura Herrmann Design
Cover Design: Laura H. Couallier, Laura Herrmann Design
Photographs: Evan J. Soldinger, except as noted

Printed in China

Pure Silver

Metal Clay Beads

Linda Kaye-Moses

Creative Publishing
international

It Was Her Nature

ARTIST: Marco Fleseri
MATERIALS: fine silver and freshwater pearls
TECHNIQUES: metal clay, hollow form construction,
hand-sculpting, cork clay core, paste-painted with added
design elements; air- and heat-dried (with hair dryer)
DIMENSIONS: 18" (45.7 cm) long

Contents

Introduction

> "Honor the past and grow into the future."
>
> —*Translation of traditional Japanese word* onkochisin

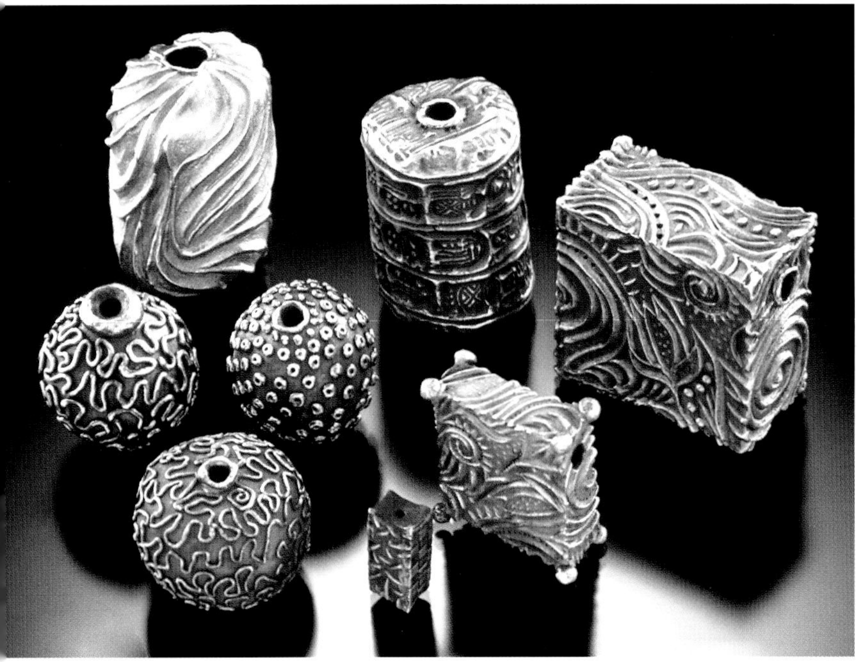

photo: Larry Sanders

Bead Collection

ARTIST: Barbara Becker Simon
MATERIALS: fine silver
TECHNIQUES: hollow form construction, patination
DIMENSIONS: largest bead: 1¼" high × 1¼" wide × ½" deep (32 × 32 × 13 mm)

This Book is about making fifteen beads with metal clay—it's not about using metal clay in all the many ways that it can be used. All of the projects are made with the brand Precious Metal Clay, or PMC, so, throughout the book, I'll refer to PMC and the formulas (fine silver PMC Standard [also called Original by some manufacturers], PMC+ and PMC3, and 22k gold PMC). All these techniques, however, can be easily adapted to the other popular brand, Art Clay. Some of the artists' examples showcased in the book are made with that material.

Why beads? The ancient human tradition of beadmaking goes back 10,000 years. The earliest jewelry was a simple string of finely cut and drilled shell disks strung by the hundreds. The labor-intensive process of making these beads is a clue to the intense interest both in personal adornment and in beads specifically. There has been and continues to be a fascination with beads that

Sphere Beads Bracelet

ARTIST: Barbara Briggs
MATERIALS: fine and sterling silver
TECHNIQUES: PMC3, hollow form construction
(Cork Clay core), tumbled, patination, polished
DIMENSIONS: 1¼" (32 mm) average diameter

photo: Barbara Briggs

transcends the millennia. This attraction, and my personal interest in beads, has lead to the creation of the beads and projects in this book.

HOW TO USE THIS BOOK

As you read and follow the directions in the projects, you'll notice that I've provided approximate metric dimensions for many of the standard measurements. It's not critical that the measurements match to the fraction, or that your samples match mine exactly, either. Only the concept and proportions for each project really matter, so don't worry about precise measurements.

This book presents materials for readers who are unfamiliar with metal clay and also for those who have experience working with it. The projects progress from beginning techniques to more advanced, to challenge beginners and experts alike. We'll explore applying color to metal, making hollow forms, making printing plates to create texture, and more. Each project also introduces new tools and techniques and is organized into logical steps to make each instruction simple to understand and follow.

So much of learning to work with metal clay is about expecting the wonderful to happen and examining possibilities. Throughout the book, you'll find images of some of the most interesting beads made by contemporary metal clay artists. This varied work displays a wide range of possible techniques and stretches the definition of what constitutes a bead.

What's most exciting is that metal clay is such a new material that the tools, equipment, techniques, and even the material, itself, are constantly being updated. The resources listed at the back of the book will help keep you abreast of those developments. You'll also find ways to see more of—and be inspired by—the work of the other metal clay artists whose beads are included in this book. The glossary will help you as you wend your way through unfamiliar terminology and the appendices provide information on different PMC formulas, firing surfaces and supports, mold-making materials, and more.

I have made every effort to make certain that the information in this book is factual and precise and that the projects will guide you to using metal clay safely. I cannot determine the safety of your work area, tools, and equipment, or if your skill levels are sufficient to work within the guidelines of the projects. You are responsible for determining that, but I have made safety notes within some of the projects and expect that you will attend to them. Here's the first one:

photo: Evan J. Soldinger

Adalisa Bead

ARTIST: Linda Kaye-Moses
MATERIALS: fine and sterling silver (chain), apatite
TECHNIQUES: metal clay, hollow form dry construction, fine silver bezel setting (fired with the bead), patination
DIMENSIONS: 1" high × 1" wide × 1" deep (25 × 25 × 25 mm)

Safety Tip

Jewelry and other precious metal objects are beautiful in their finished state, but be aware that the processes for creating them using metal clay and other techniques can present some safety hazards. Safe procedures are offered throughout the project instructions in this book. Please exercise caution when following the instructions and, whenever you are unsure of risk, rely on common sense. Ultimately, you are responsible for protecting yourself.

Mosaic

ARTIST: Hadar Jacobson
MATERIALS: fine silver, copper, brass, bronze
TECHNIQUES: metal clay, soldering
DIMENSIONS: 1⅝" × 1" × ¼" (42 × 25 × 6 mm)

photo: Hadar Jacobson

A VERY BRIEF HISTORY OF METAL CLAY

In 1995, metal clay began to be available outside Japan, where the material was developed. In that same year, an article appeared in *Modern Jewelry* ("A New Kind of Gold: Who Kneads It?") that described a new material that promised to revolutionize the process of making jewelry—Precious Metal Clay.

Initially, there were a few experimental workshops and master classes, and, in 1996, metal clay became available to the general public in the United States. Soon, the first classes and workshops were offered to the general public, and since then, these have multiplied into hundreds all around the world (in 2002, I taught three workshops in New Zealand).

Since 1996, there have been numerous books written about metal clay, a number of which are listed on pages 152–153. More classes and workshops are offered, enabling more and more people to discover this revolutionary material. Although the material has not been available for very long, there have also been some great exhibitions of artists' work in metal clay. It's still such a very new material that we have only just begun to imagine the many ways that it can be used. (For a more in-depth history, see PMC Decade in Further Reading, page 152).

photo: Larry Sanders

Leafy Ball with Cap

ARTIST: Jean Wydra
MATERIALS: fine silver, vitreous enamel
TECHNIQUES: metal clay, wet construction over wax-coated foam core, enameling
DIMENSIONS: 1½" (38 mm) diameter

Working with Metal CLAY

Metal Clay

is precious metal in a claylike form that can be shaped with your fingers and other tools, fired in a kiln or torch-fired, and finished and polished as you would any precious metal. Potters and ceramicists who work with earthen clays say that unfired metal clay feels much like porcelain clay.

Metal clay is one of the most user-friendly methods of making precious metal objects. If you're making an object in fresh metal clay that you find you don't like, you can just roll it up and begin again. Happily, every day, I learn unique and innovative techniques—and many times I have learned unexpected and delightful techniques from my students. There is something about the material that inspires the people who work with it to dare processes that other media would not encourage.

In this chapter, you'll find answers to many questions that beginners may have about metal

Open Reversible Bead
ARTIST: Linda Kaye-Moses
MATERIALS: fine silver
TECHNIQUE: dry construction
DIMENSIONS: 1⅛" (29 mm) square

Large Tubular Bead
ARTIST: Linda Kaye-Moses
MATERIAL: fine silver
TECHNIQUE: dry construction
DIMENSIONS: 1½" × ½" diameter (33 mm × 12 mm)

clay. Don't get bogged down in all the information, however. As you work through the projects, keep in mind Hildegard von Bingen's admonition, "Be not lax in celebrating … be ablaze with enthusiasm." Some of this information might not be useful to you until you're working with the material, but it is organized, as much as is possible, to reflect the order in which you will need it.

WHAT IS METAL CLAY?

Metal clay is composed of micron-fine particles of precious metal (as fine as talcum powder). The particles are bound in a nontoxic organic binding agent (binder) combined with a small amount of water. There are two brands of precious metal clay, both manufactured in Japan: Art Clay (from Aida Chemical Industries) and Precious Metal Clay or PMC (from Mitsubishi Materials).

For the projects in this book, I worked exclusively with PMC. Many of its properties are similar to the properties of the various formulas of Art Clay and, in most cases, the two brands are nearly interchangeable. Some artists work with both brands, and others artists, like me, prefer one or the other.

Metal clay is very responsive to textures and shaping and also to many traditional metalsmithing techniques. For example, it can be hollow-formed, press-molded, stamped, rolled, lightly forged, enameled, patinated, engraved, carved, set with stones, and slip-painted. We'll explore many of these techniques in this book—but for every technique discussed, ten new ones are evolving every day.

Lump of fresh metal clay (PMC3) and packaging

Samples of PMC Standard (also known as Original), PMC+, and PMC3, showing relative shrinkage: The upper row is unfired/dry, the middle row is fired/unpolished, and the lower row is tumble polished.

Before metal clay is fired, the material is formed and fully dried. You can store a dried metal clay object almost indefinitely. Although the binder is organic and may, while wet, respond to mold in the atmosphere, the object is normally static and so can be fired whenever convenient.

To transform the clay into its final metallic form, metal clay requires a firing or heating process. The firing process brings the metal clay to temperatures lower than the melting temperatures of the metal in the clay, allowing the binder to burn away and leaving only a precious metal object. The metals in the clay can be either fine silver or an alloy of gold or bronze. During the firing process, the metal particles, which had been originally separated by the binder, come together, sinter (bond without melting), and shrink, forming an object that is light, durable, and precious.

ABOUT SHRINKAGE

The rate of shrinkage is based on the percentage of binder and water in the specific type or formula of metal clay. The quantity and weight of precious metal in metal clay remains constant, although, after the binder has burned away during firing, the metal object becomes smaller.

One method for getting used to gauging the shrinkage of metal clay is to make sample "tiles" in each of the formulas, in a range of thicknesses. These don't have to be very large—perhaps a prefired size of ½" (12 mm) square. Note the dimensions of the tile at three stages: while still moist, after drying, and after firing. Eventually, you'll develop an intuitive understanding of the shrinkage rates, but until then, the tiles will help you determine how large to make your work.

THE FORMULAS AND THEIR PROPERTIES

Fine silver Precious Metal Clay is made in three formulas: PMC Standard (sometimes called Original), PMC+, and PMC3. There's only one formula of 22k yellow gold PMC. (Aura 22, made by the manufacturer of Precious Metal Clay, is a paintable 22k gold.) For firing temperatures and schedules for all these formulas, see pages 144–145.

All three silver formulas can be fired at 1650°F (900°C). Because that temperature is below the melting point of fine silver, which is 1762°F (960°C), the metal clay object will fire safely. PMC+ and PMC3 can also be fired at three different temperatures for three different lengths of time. The longer the firing time, the stronger the final product. The metal won't necessarily be weak if you fire at the recommended lower temperatures and shorter durations. It just won't be as strong as it would be if you fired at the highest temperature for the longest duration.

The lower temperatures and shorter duration formulas allow you to fire some precious stones, glass, sterling silver findings, or other sensitive materials (such as beach stones and ceramic elements) embedded in the metal clay, without damage. Firing below the lowest suggested temperatures will result in a weak and incompletely sintered object.

Two Basic Rules

1. Unfired, wet metal clay is somewhat sticky and so must be handled with lubricated hands, tools, and work surfaces.

2. Metal clay must be fired at the suggested temperatures for each formula and at least for the minimum suggested duration.

WARNING: Never work with aluminum tools or work surfaces. Contact between metal clay and aluminum will contaminate the clay and cause discoloration, warping, brittleness, and incomplete sintering.

All three fine silver metal clays—without sensitive embedded materials—can be fired for two hours or longer (although not much happens to the fired object after two hours). It's also possible to fire the 22k gold PMC for longer firing times. The only truly critical consideration is to avoid exceeding the melting points of the silver or gold.

The projects in the book use each of the PMC formulas. I have suggested firing at the highest temperature for the longest duration to ensure strong, durable beads. The specific formula you'll need is listed in the materials box for each project.

METAL CLAY SLIP

Slip is metal clay with extra water, in other words, a more fluid, thinner metal clay. Slip is the great joiner. It's used to join or "glue" two or more pieces

Metal clay slip
(with jar and syringe)

of an unfired metal clay object. It's also the great "repair guy"—used to repair flaws, cracks, holes, and bumps in the metal clay surface. It's also used for slip-painting (see page 20).

You can buy ready-made slip or make it yourself. PMC+ slip and PMC3 slip are available ready-made. Although the manufacturer does not provide a ready-made slip specifically for PMC Standard or for 22k gold PMC, PMC+ slip, or PMC3 slip can be used with all the formulas.

To make slip yourself, you can simply add water to any of the formulas of fresh metal clay or reconstitute sanding dust or dried bits. Just add water to the material, a little bit at a time, until it is absorbed so the clay has a usable consistency. Stir and smear to blend in any chunks and voilà—you've made slip! Store it in a jar with a snug lid.

Use homemade PMC Standard slip only on PMC Standard. Store each slip formula in separate, labeled containers for easy identification.

PMC3 slip can be combined with lavender or other essential oil to make an even stronger slip. This type of slip is called an intense slip, and it's useful for fired metal clay that needs repairs, has broken, or will have new parts attached. It can also be used on unfired metal clay, if necessary.

The recipe for intense slip is 25 to 35 drops of lavender oil or another essential oil to one full jar of PMC3 slip (about 15 grams of homemade slip). Stir together to make a thick, strong slip. You might need to add a little bit of water to make the slip spreadable.

REHYDRATING CLAY

Metal clay will air-dry while you are working with it. Keep a small water mister handy. When you compress a lump of metal clay and see small cracks appearing at the edge, spray the water in the air and move the drying clay through that mist. You don't want to soak the clay. You just want to moisten it a little. Oil your hands with olive oil or another lubricant (see page 17). Roll the moistened clay in your oiled hands to evenly mix in the water.

While you work the metal clay, you'll cut off excess pieces or lumps to shape the forms you're making. As soon as possible, return these pieces to the plastic wrap in their sealable package. If you think they've begun to dry, add a small drop of water on the surface of the metal clay. Then wrap the clay in plastic wrap and put it in the package with a small piece of moistened paper towel.

Making Flexible Metal Clay

Some objects require a flexible form of metal clay—for example, for a braid, a woven element, or bezels for stone-setting. This form might be useful, for example, when making the Ribbon Bead project (see page 68), which employs the metal clay extruder. In these cases, it's helpful to hyperhydrate and slow the drying of PMC+ and PMC3. Hadar Jacobson (see page 155) and others have developed the process of using glycerin to lengthen the drying time, to allow the metal clay to remain flexible and be manipulated without cracking. This process is also very useful in arid climates or where there is a strong airflow, such as air-conditioning, in the work area. Jeanette Landenwitch, the director of the Precious Metal Clay Guild, uses olive oil. A commercially available product called Extender serves a similar purpose, but plain glycerin works just fine.

The Ribbon Bead can be made with flexible metal clay (see page 68).

Tubular Bead #1 has a wrapped and curved surface. To prevent the bead from developing cracks, make it pliable by moistening it with glycerin (see page 52).

Depending on the quantity of metal clay you are using, add a very tiny amount of glycerin (for a full package, add 3 to 5 drops). If you add too much, the clay won't be usable. This glycerin/metal clay combination must be air-dried. It cannot be heat-dried.

Roll out the metal clay into a very thin sheet on your work surface. Spread the drops of glycerin evenly on the surface of the metal clay with a clean shaper or your fingertip. Roll the metal clay into a ball. Place a sheet of plastic wrap or a small plastic bag on top of the ball and again roll the metal clay into a very thin sheet. Reroll about five times to complete the amalgamation. Allow the clay to "rest" for a minimum of 30 minutes or overnight to allow the glycerin to evenly combine with the metal clay.

Sometimes you may want to make a thin, dry element pliable—to add to a curved surface, for example, in the Tubular Bead #1 project (see page 50). If the element is fully dried and relatively thin, simply lightly moisten the back with water, wait a few minutes, check for pliability, and, when it's pliable, manipulate it as you wish.

You can also use *a very little bit* of glycerin to moisten clay that is either dry or partially dry. The glycerin allows you to manipulate the clay without its cracking and without losing any textures. Again, air-dry.

If you instead want to keep the clay on your worktable for easier access, place the clay alongside a small piece of moistened sponge under a small glass (such as a shot glass). The clay won't dry out and will be handy when you're ready to work with it. Don't use this method to store the clay indefinitely, however.

Sometimes the metal clay may seem to be getting more than a bit dry—especially true with PMC+ and PMC3, and sometimes PMC Standard, too. Adding more water is a good solution, but adding too much can be messy, making the clay a bit too sticky. If you need to rehydrate PMC+ and PMC3, add only a very small drop of water at a time and knead it into the clay. Then wrap the clay in plastic wrap and set it aside to allow the water to be absorbed completely.

A quicker method is to roll the moistened metal clay between a sheet of plastic wrap or a plastic bag and the work surface (the thickness doesn't matter). Then scrape the clay up into a lump with a tissue blade (see page 28) and roll it out again under the plastic wrap. Repeat this three or four times, then roll the clay into a ball, ready for use.

If you leave an open package of metal clay unsealed, the material may become completely dry. Fortunately, it's easy to reconstitute the material.

First, break the clay into small pieces. You can use a tissue blade to break it. If the clay is very hard, put it into two small plastic baggies, one inside the other, place it on a hard surface, and hit it with a hammer. Continue to break up the small pieces, with the tissue blade or with a small electric spice grinder (dedicated to just this purpose).

Place the pieces of metal clay in a small, sealable container and add a few drops of water. Remember that fresh metal clay is about 10 percent water, so add the water a few drops at a time until your clay has reached the consistency you want. If it gets too soupy, leave the container open for a while, but check it often. Stir the mixture occasionally, and eventually you will have salvaged your metal clay.

WORK SURFACES

Working with metal clay requires a smooth, easy-to-use work surface. There are many options: a nonstick cooking sheet, a Plexiglas sheet, plastic-coated playing cards, ¼" (6 mm)-thick plate glass—any waterproof, durable surface that will allow you to roll out and trim a sheet of metal clay without flaws, can accept lubrication, and can be washed occasionally.

My favorite is a 4 × 5" (10 x 12 cm) sheet of tempered plate glass no less than ¼" (6 mm) thick. Go to a custom glass supplier/installer and have them cut the piece and polish the edges. I like to use tempered glass for a number of reasons. It's durable and won't shatter, but if you need to replace it, it's readily available. The surface is very smooth. It's small enough to rotate easily on the worktable so I can view and work the metal clay—and it's easy to lift to check the underside of clay I've rolled out. On the downside, it does need to be lubricated with oil, but this is a minor drawback.

LUBRICATION

Metal clay is sticky, to varying degrees, depending on the specific formula. So, before working with it, your hands, tools, and work surfaces need to be lightly lubricated. In fact, anything that comes in contact with the clay needs to be lubricated. Several lubricants are available.

My personal favorite is olive oil, for a number of reasons: availability, absence of fragrance, ease of use, effectiveness—and it also moisturizes my hands. To prevent spillage on the worktable, I keep the oil in a shallow porcelain saucer with a piece of a kitchen sponge in it. Some suppliers offer small storage containers. I drizzle a bit of olive oil onto the sponge, adding more when necessary. As I work, I swipe a finger or tool across the sponge when needed. Other types of lubricants include Badger Balm (available unscented), ClayMate, and Slik.

TEXTURES

One of the beauties of metal clay is that it so readily accepts textures of all kinds. Almost anything that you want to press into it, press onto it, or press it into will leave a mark in the surface of the clay. The shrinkage of all formulas of metal clay brings any texture into sharper detail, especially PMC Standard, which shrinks the most.

Metal clay can be scribed (marked with a pointed tool), carved, forged (shaped with a hammer), or rolled. It can accept rubber stamp designs, patterns from rocks, lace, hair combs, photopolymer plates, carved polymer sheet, carved printing blocks, and more. When I taught in New Zealand, I incorporated seaweed, tree roots, even patterns on glass shower stall doors into the workshop demonstrations.

You can re-create imagery very accurately, but some textures, when acquired by metal clay, defy identification—and that's a good thing.

> ### Tip
> If you are using olive oil as the lubricant, cut a piece of a kitchen sponge into a 1" (2.5 cm) square. Place the sponge in a small saucer or directly on your worktable. Pour a small amount of oil on the sponge and allow it to soak in. Then, whenever you need lubricant, just swipe a tool or your fingers across the surface of the sponge.

Textures are just the starting point. After the metal clay sheet is imprinted, it can be altered in any number of ways.

BEAD CORES

Some metal clay beads have a solid core and some are hollow. Hollow metal clay beads may require an interior support while being constructed and some also need support while being fired. The supporting bead cores are called armatures, whether fired with the bead or not.

The choice of core and armature materials is limited only by your imagination, but here are some that you might want to try. Not all of these materials are used in the projects, but all can be used with metal clay.

Core and Armature Materials That Can Be Fired

- bread dough
- blueberries, grapes, and other small round fruit
- papier-mâché
- prepared dry cereals
- Creative Paper Clay (a paperlike material)
- some snack foods and chips
- wax
- wet/dry emery paper or other coated paper
- mesh sanding sheet (for drywall)
- Cork Clay or Wood Clay
- bisque beads
- carved soft firebrick
- paper
- pasta
- copper screening
- plaster of paris

Core and Armature Materials That Cannot Be Fired

- hard-boiled eggs or plastic Easter eggs
- round lightbulbs
- baked polymer clay forms

Cork Clay and Wood Clay are commercial modeling materials. Either one would be an adequate substitute for the stone armature used in a few of the projects in this book—for example, the Vessel Bead (see page 116) and the Belted Dome Bead (see page 92). Both materials are nontoxic, although ventilation is required during firing because of smoke. Both also need to be completely dried after forming and before applying the metal clay to them. Drying overnight, and sometimes longer, is required. Wood Clay has a finer texture and is easier to carve when dry.

MAKING MOLDS

Another quality of metal clays is their ability to be press-molded. What is press molding? In this process, a soft material (the metal clay) is pressed into a mold and assumes the shape and image of the mold. The mold can be any of a number of different materials, but requires two essential qualities: it must be capable of reproducing a good image and it must permit easy release of the metal clay. Any material that sticks to metal clay would have to be adapted to prevent the stickiness.

Plaster of paris, for example, is a good mold material, but is very water absorbent. The metal clay will adhere to the bare surface of the mold and will produce a flawed image, if any at all. The best way to use a plaster of paris mold is to lightly varnish the surface, sealing the material and preventing the metal clay from sticking.

Many ready-made molds—from small baking molds to those designed for polymer clay—can be used with metal clay, including molds marketed specifically for metal clay. You can also make your own molds, as described in the Mold-Formed Bead project on page 56. There are two primary steps to making a handmade mold. First, select an object as a model to reproduce—it can be anything from a button to a beetle to a shell. Then select an appropriate mold-making material to reproduce the model (for more about mold materials for metal clay, see page 147).

The Vessel Bead (*left*) and the Belted Dome Bead (*center*) were made with a smooth stone armature. The Mold-Formed Bead (*right*) is shaped in a custom-made mold, as described on page 56.

Working with Water

When working with metal clay, you need water for several purposes. The water you work with should be relatively free of minerals. The standard recommendation is to use distilled water, but in my studios, I've used both water from a municipal water supply and water from an artesian well. Neither type seems to have affected the metal clay in any measurable way, but, if you suspect that your water is loaded with minerals (hard water), consider using distilled water when you work with metal clay.

Here are some of the ways you'll use water with metal clay:

- To rehydrate partially dried or dried metal clay
- To thin metal clay for slip-painting
- To make homemade slip from metal clay sanding dust or dried bits
- To "reactivate" the surface or other areas on an object, to smooth or refine those areas
- To "reactivate" a spot on one metal clay object, to join it more securely to another
- To make a dried sheet of metal clay pliable, usually to make it conform to a curved surface

JOINING DRY METAL CLAY PARTS

Most often, I join only fully dried metal clay parts. I moisten a very small section of the areas to be joined to "reactivate" the metal clay, actually creating a little spot of slip. (If you scratch that moistened area lightly with a scribe or needle, you'll bring up that slip.) I work with either a paintbrush and water or a filled waterbrush. The paintbrush technique is simple, but you need to keep a small cup of water on the worktable, which can lead to spills. The waterbrush is more efficient.

I add slip to one of the parts and carefully bring the parts together. The parts can be fragile in their dry or greenware (unfired) state, depending on their thickness. While pressing them together, I rotate them back and forth, one or more times, then return them to their appropriate position.

I don't worry about cleaning up any excess slip that may ooze out of the joint, although I may use a color shaper or clay shaper to clean up some of it. It's easier to clean the joint after it has dried. I join successive parts, drying thoroughly after each join.

SLIP-PAINTING

Slip-painting is just what it sounds like. You simply apply metal clay slip to the surface of a supporting model with a small watercolor or oil-paint brush. Then allow the slip to dry and paint on additional layers—generally, no less than ten and as many as twelve. The finished object closely resembles the original supporting model.

This process offers many possibilities. You can slip-paint a core of plant pods, leaves, folded paper (origami designs, for example), twigs, dried flowers, and so on. Your models should have deep textures and interesting forms. The only essential requirement is that the core object should burn out completely and safely during the firing process. Avoid all plastics and Styrofoam. Even though they burn out, their fumes are toxic to breathe and pollute the atmosphere.

DRYING METHODS

The least complicated method for drying metal clay is to air-dry it on a clean surface. You must air-dry those pieces that will have wax or other inclusions that will melt if the clay is heated or if the piece may warp if it dries too quickly.

Most of the time, however, I'm too impatient to wait for a piece to air-dry and prefer to heat-dry my pieces, if appropriate. There are several types of drying tools: hair dryers, small electric mug warmers (also sold as potpourri or candle warmers), dehydrators (usually sold for dehydrating vegetables and fruits), small convection ovens, or on a kiln pad on top of an already warm kiln.

Never use a microwave for drying metal clay. Always preheat a mug warmer, dehydrator, oven, or trinket kiln before you begin to work with the metal clay. Hair dryers are the most readily available drying tool. I use one to dry slip-painting when I can't put the piece down.

Electric mug warmers are the dryers of choice for me when I'm making just a few pieces. These little appliances are small enough to keep on my worktable, along with all the other stuff that has to be there. They heat at just the right temperature to dry metal clay swiftly (some even have two temperatures to permit slower drying if warping is a possibility). Place a small screen of copper mesh on the surface of the warmer, and the clay will dry more slowly. I admit that I've never purchased a new mug warmer. They seem to show up fairly frequently at local thrift stores and secondhand shops, and I've acquired quite a few.

The dehydrator used for drying metal clay has a heat source and several levels of trays. I choose a dehydrator when I need to dry many pieces at once. Dehydrators are readily available and dry metal clay quickly and evenly.

The drawback for me is that they generally take up too much horizontal space, which is at a premium in my studio.

Small convection ovens are a good alternative to toaster ovens, because the temperature is more controllable and more even. They are the most expensive drying devices, however, and not necessarily the most convenient. If you use a convection oven or a toaster oven, there are two cautionary notes. First, dedicate the oven for working with art materials only, not food. Second, if you use the same oven for drying metal clay and baking polymer clay, be aware that you cannot heat the oven above the manufacturer's recommended temperature for curing polymer clay. If you do, you run the risk of burning any polymers that have been deposited inside the oven. The recommended temperature for drying metal clay in an oven is 250°F (120°C). Use an oven thermometer to ensure that you don't exceed that temperature.

If your metal clay kiln is warm (or hot), you can set a kiln pad on top and place the metal clay piece on the pad to dry it. I would not recommend this method with small trinket-style kilns, as high temperatures might melt the lid, but it's a fine way to utilize the warmth from a large, box-style kiln.

You may store the dry, formed metal clay for a day, a week, or longer before firing it in the kiln.

One type of metal clay kiln

In its unfired, or greenware, state, it's fragile, so be sure to store it in a protected spot.

FIRING

Metal clay is ready to be fired only when it is completely dry. The easy way to tell is to put the object on a sheet of clean glass or mirror. After 15 to 20 seconds, lift the object from the surface. If the object is not dry, there will be condensation on the glass surface. Continue to allow your object to dry until it passes this condensation test.

Metal clay can be fired in a number of ways. It can be torch-fired, kiln-fired (computer or manually controlled), fired in a small pot-type kiln, in a trinket-style kiln, and even on a gas stovetop. When I teach and in my own work, I kiln-fire in a computer-controlled kiln. The only true drawback to a computer-controlled kiln is the cost, but it has many advantages:

- It holds at the correct temperature for the correct duration.

- It can be programmed to an almost infinite number of requirements, limited only by the upper temperature that the kiln can achieve without burning out the elements.

- Its controls permit me to focus on other activities (making more pieces, gardening, eating, taking a walk). I don't have to monitor the kiln or work to maintain the correct temperature, as I do with other methods.

- It can also be used for different media techniques such as fusing glass and enameling.

- Most important, it will consistently and perfectly sinter the metal clay.

If you don't want to invest in this type of kiln, check with a local guild or art school for access to one (see pages 151–152).

Some formulas of metal clay (PMC+ and PMC3) can be fired with a gas-fired torch (such as butane or air/acetylene). I do not recommend or teach this method, because I'm not convinced that the metal completely sinters to achieve its greatest strength. Metal clay manufacturers, however, consider the torch-firing method as adequate for sintering. There is extensive information available about torch-firing methods through metal clay guilds and on the Internet.

Torch-Firing Precious Metal Clay

Torch-firing is appropriate only for small objects. Be sure the object is completely dry before firing.

1. Place a soldering block or firebrick on a fireproof surface near a source of active ventilation.

2. Place the metal clay object on the block or brick. Turn on the ventilation.

3. Light the torch.

4. Hold the torch above the object, with the torch flame vertical and the tip of the flame's cone about ¾" (19.5 mm) away from the object.

5. After about one minute, as the binder burns away, the piece will be enveloped in a soft flame. When the binder has burned away, the flame will go out.

6. After another minute, the piece will glow red, then become a very bright and shiny red. At that point, begin timing with a clock or stopwatch.

7. Continue to fire the piece to hold this color as follows: for PMC+, at least 5 minutes; for PMC3, 2 minutes.

8. When the time is up, turn off the torch.

9. Allow the piece to cool to room temperature.

Firing Flat Forms

There are many options for surfaces on which to fire a flat form: soft firebrick, asbestos-free soldering pads, and pottery/ceramic kiln furniture. I use all three of these surfaces. I'm still using pieces of firebrick that I cut ten years ago, even though they've cracked into smaller pieces. For more information, see page 145.

Firing Curved and Hollow Forms

Curved and hollow forms, such as beads, require special firing support to prevent the weight of the material from collapsing, or slumping, the bead. Fill the container, or sagger—which should be unglazed terra-cotta (such as a small flowerpot or flowerpot saucer), stainless steel, or another heat-resistant, nonreactive material—with a powdery or grainy heat-resistant material, such as alumina hydrate or vermiculite. Place the bead in the container for firing. "Pillows" of the thermal insulation material Kaowool can also be used for curved clay forms (see page 146).

Quenching, or Cooling

You can remove a fired metal clay object from the kiln while the object is still hot (as long as there are no glass or gemstone inclusions) if you wear heavy gloves and use a pair of long-handled tweezers or even a pair of barbecue tongs. Immediately immerse the object in cold water in a heatproof container (a stainless-steel bowl or pan) to cool it rapidly or quench it. Cooling a piece quickly is not a necessary process, but it does speed the cooling process and will not damage the object.

MAKING REPAIRS

You can use slip or fresh metal clay to repair an unfired silver bead, depending on the size of the area that needs repair. Slip is generally all you need to repair a small crack or hole; for a larger gap, you may need to add fresh clay. In both cases, work with a shaper as you make the repairs.

To repair a fired silver bead that has developed cracks or gaps during the firing, you need fresh metal clay. Again, use a shaper to apply the clay and use more clay than looks proportional (remember, the new clay will shrink; the bead already has). Smooth all seams where the fresh clay meets the fired object. Some repairs may require a bit of creativity due to textures or patterns in the fired object.

If a hole appears in a piece after firing, you may be able to repair it by squeezing additional fresh metal clay through the hole and smoothing it on the other side. Again, use more than you think you might need, because it will shrink when refired. Repair fired metal clay that has broken apart with intense (essential oil–based) slip, described on page 14.

REFINING AN UNFIRED SURFACE

Before firing metal clay, you will need to refine the surface of your piece(s) so that it is as close as possible to what you would like the fired piece to look like. You'll notice the instructions for making the projects always include an instruction to refine and sand your bead as the last step before firing.

Check the bead for lumps, bumps, and cracks. Repair the cracks with fresh metal clay or slip, depending on the size of the crack. Smooth lumps and bumps by adding a little water to the area and rubbing with a shaper.

Work with a 220-grit wet/dry emery paper or a coarse-grit salon board (abrasive boards used to sand and file artificial fingernails, available in a range of grits). Refine all edges or corners of the bead, or parts of the bead, before joining the parts together. Begin sanding to remove any scratches on the surface of the bead. Sand back and forth until you have achieved a homogeneous surface.

Next, sand across the previous sanding direction with a finer-grit board or emery paper. Continue this process, alternating the direction of the sanding, until you no longer see any fine lines from the most recent round of sanding. Remember, if your bead has a texture, you don't want to remove it by sanding too aggressively. Then continue sanding with microfinishing papers (see page 143) to achieve a very smooth, shiny surface.

FINISHING

Once the bead is fired, the surface of the bead looks matte and more like pottery than metal. These are the metal oxides, deposited on the surface during the firing. The first step in finishing your bead is to remove those oxides.

Design Tip

Choosing the finish for your bead offers you a way to make the bead uniquely your own. It doesn't have to look like anybody else's. The finish only has to please one person—you!

Project beads after tumble-finishing

Removing Oxides

Add a little liquid dishwashing detergent to the moistened bristles of a jeweler's brass brush and vigorously brush the bead, remoistening the brush every so often. This process should remove the matte surface.

You could also use a product called Scotch-Brite, made by 3M, to quickly and easily remove surface oxides and produce a first finish on metal. Cut it into 1-inch (25 mm) squares and mount squares on a screw mandrel, three at a time, and insert the mandrel in a rotary tool (such as a flex-shaft machine or a Dremel). You might like the finish this method produces and decide to use it as the final finish for your pieces.

Sometimes it's difficult to get into the recesses of a deeply textured surface with the brass brush. If so, the easiest option is to put the piece into a tumbler. A magnetic tumbler is the quickest and therefore the most efficient, but a rotary tumbler will also get the job done, although it will take a little longer.

If you want to remove the remaining oxides by hand, you can burnish the hard-to-get recesses with small, ball-tipped dental tools, compressing the surface. Sometimes tumbling will reveal areas that still need more attention. Generally, I use a flex-shaft machine (or other type of rotary tool) and 3M's Scotch-Brite Radial Bristle Discs, in a range of grits, to correct any problems. I don't usually recommend one brand over another, but these discs really do a terrific job.

Patination

If, after you've brushed and burnished, you've achieved a finish on your bead that you like, you don't have to go any further—but if you want to, here are some ideas (you'll learn more about these in the individual projects).

I prefer my work to have a patina because it enhances the recesses of a textured surface. I always use liver of sulfur, a darkening chemical for silver (see page 148). To achieve the final finish, I next use a flex-shaft machine (or other rotary tool) and 3M Scotch-Brite Radial Bristle Discs in a micron-fine grit. This finish will brighten up the high spots and leave the recesses dark, which is what I aim for. Last, I vigorously rub the piece with a polishing cloth.

There are so many ways to finish precious metals. The choices depend on the look you want to achieve, from bright, mirrored finish to soft, brushed look to dark, matte. Refer to the books on jewelry making on pages 152–153 to learn more.

Polishing

You can achieve a bright surface on precious metal by using increasingly finer abrasives embedded in a greasy binder, generally available in stick or block form. Some abrasive types include jeweler's rouges, Zam, bobbing compound, Tripoli, White Diamond, and Fabulustre. Abrasives are either applied to muslin or felt wheels that are mounted on large polishing machines or are attached to a handheld rotary tool (such as a flex-shaft machine or a Dremel). As you hold the metal object against

Safety Tip

Breathing the dust from abrasive compounds is hazardous, so you'll need to work with a respirator and adequate venting. You'll also need a sturdy face shield when using polishing machines or rotary tools.

A Low-Tech Patination Process

There's a low-tech way to patina fine silver, sterling silver, and copper. All you need is a hard-boiled egg. This process is not as controllable, predictable, or fast as working with liver of sulfur (see page 148), but the results can be interesting.

1. Place your metal object and a peeled hard-boiled egg in a jar and cover tightly (an older egg will give off more sulfur, the chemical that produces the desired reaction).

2. Set the jar aside in a warm environment, checking the intensity of the patina from time to time.

3. When the object is the color you want, remove it from the jar The color may need overnight to develop. Complete your finish as you would when using liver of sulfur. Discard the egg.

the spinning wheels, the abrasive polishes the surface of the metal. You can also hand-polish with cloths that contain similar abrasives. Clean up the object after polishing with an ultrasonic cleaner or a good degreasing agent and a soft bristled brush. (See pages 151–152 for a list of places that offer workshops or classes on finishing and polishing.)

Tools and Supplies

Here is an overview of some of the tools and supplies you'll need when working with metal clay. A complete list of materials is also included with each of the projects in the book.

▲ Assorted brass jeweler's brushes

These wooden-handled brushes have short brass bristles imbedded in the handle. The bristles are softer than those on the type of metal-bristled brushes found in hardware stores. With these brushes, you'll begin the process of adding a finish to fired metal clay objects.

▲ Metal clay tools

1. mug warmer and tweezers, **2.** small mirror (for testing dryness of clay), **3.** packages of the three types of Precious Metal Clay, **4.** jar of metal clay slip, **5.** syringe for metal clay, **6.** two shapers, **7.** fine-line marker, **8.** soft lead pencil, **9.** taped playing cards, **10.** two scribes, **11.** needles, **12.** plastic roller, **13.** tempered glass work surface, **14.** metal ruler, **15.** small sponge for olive oil, **16.** waterbrush, **17.** paintbrushes, **18.** sanding/finishing supplies (salon boards, wet/dry emery paper, polishing sheets)

▲ Assorted burnishers

Burnishers for metal clay are generally smooth, polished, steel tools that impart a bright, smooth surface on fired silver or gold objects. You can work with specifically designed jeweler's burnishers, the backs of dull butter knives, or similar types of tools.

▲ Tissue blades (with taped safety edge)

Tissue blades are long, narrow rectangles of very thin steel. One long side of the tool is sharpened to razor sharpness. It can sometimes be difficult to tell which is the sharp edge, when picking up the tool. For this reason, I tape the dull edge with bright-colored electrical tape, making a very visible reminder of which edge to hold.

▲ Assorted X-Acto knives and art knives

X-Acto knives, or art knives, have two parts: a handle and a blade. The blades are available in many shapes and sizes. The shape I prefer to use for metal clay work is a long, narrow triangle. The blade is inserted in the chuck located at one end of the handle, and the chuck is then tightened to hold the blade securely. When using an art knife, be sure to move the blade in the direction away from your body and hands.

◀ Assorted cutters

Circle cutters are available as spring-loaded punches in graduated sizes (one brand is Klay Kutters). Brass tubing, also available in graduated sizes and in several diameters, can be cut to short lengths with a jeweler's saw and sanded smooth. Cutting good circles in metal clay can also be done with a circle template or other circular object (small pill containers, coffee stirrers, drinking straws, drinking glasses) and a needle tool or a scribe.

Decorative cutters are available in graduated sizes and many different shapes, including squares, triangles, stars, hearts, ovals, and teardrops. Zigzag cutters, which are wavy-edged, are used to decoratively trim metal clay sheet or to impress a pattern on the sheet.

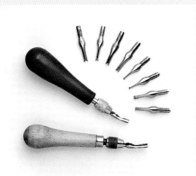

▲ Assorted linoleum carvers and blades

Linoleum carvers are for carving soft rubber-like sheets or blocks that work like printing blocks to add patterns and textures onto the surface of metal clay. Sheet and blocks come in a range of sizes and thicknesses. I order a large sheet and cut it into smaller sections.

The carvers consist of wooden or plastic handles with a fitting for interchangeable cutting blades that come in many shapes. I find V-shaped blades the most useful but I keep other blade shapes in case I need to remove material in different ways.

▲ Cutting and filing tools

(from the left, counterclockwise) fine-tip scissors, side cutters, needle file, wax file, assorted pin vises and drill bits, assorted circle cutters, tissue blade (with tape on safe edge), art knife, opened paper clip (for carving out wet clay)

▲ Assorted plastic rollers

Metal clay sheet is the basis for almost every object you might want to make in metal clay. You'll also need smooth, plastic rollers to roll it out. They are available ready-made from many suppliers, in Plexiglas or polyvinyl chloride (PVC). I suggest a maximum length of 5 to 8 inches (12.7 to 20.3 cm).

To make your own roller, cut a piece of PVC pipe to length. Use emery paper to sand the end, but wet the paper before sanding. Always wet-sand plastics to avoid releasing and inhaling particles and dust. Toss the emery paper in the trash when you're finished.

◀ Assorted salon (sanding) boards

I recommend salon boards in the materials list for every project in the book. These sanding abrasives come in easy-to-use sizes and are mounted on each side of a foam core. They were designed for manicuring artificial fingernails, but they use the same range of abrasive grits that are used for sanding metals and dried metal clay.

▲ PMC and standard rulers

Standard rulers are useful for measuring and refining your designs. Steel rulers are durable and easy to keep clean. PMC rulers have measurements that help you to determine the postfiring shrinkage of a metal clay object.

▼ Emery papers

Emery paper is water-resistant paper with a surface of abrasive grit in a range that permits fine finishing of dried metal clay and metal surfaces. You can use wet/dry emery paper on unfired metal clay. You can use it wet or dry on metal.

◀ Thickness guides

To roll out metal clay to a uniform thickness, it's helpful to have a thickness guide. The guide will lift the roller to a specific height that will correspond to the desired final thickness of the metal clay.

I make my own thickness guides by stacking plastic-coated playing cards to varying thickness and taping the cards together. I position a numbered card appropriate to the number of cards in the stack on top, so I can readily see how many cards are in each stack. When the cards become too soiled, I discard them and start with a fresh set of cards. Look for playing cards that are smooth, with no texture on the surface. You could also use plastic strips cut from deli container lids, plastic notebook covers, or similar materials.

There are a number of ready-made guides (spacers and slats) in a range of thicknesses, all of which work very efficiently, such as these guides, at left, from Whole Lotta Whimsy.

▲ Scribe and needle

Scribes are sharp-pointed tools for making marks and for cleaning off excess metal clay or slip. As substitutes, you can use large sewing needles, dental tools, or similar implements. These tools can also be used to draw designs in the surface of metal clay.

Assorted shapers

Color or clay shapers are wonderful tools for working metal clay. They are silicone-tipped, with a paintbrush-style handle. Shaper tips are available in a range of sizes, hardnesses, and shapes. You can use them to smooth, apply slip, clean up slip, moisten clay, lightly carve, make depressions, and more. They're the best multitasking tools you can have when working metal clay. I prefer tapered-point shapes, both soft and firm, small and large, but it's helpful to have a range of sizes, hardnesses, and shapes at hand.

Waterbrushes

A waterbrush offers an efficient method for dispensing water on your worktable, without the danger of spilling water on your work. It is a self-contained tube of water with a brush on the end. With a slight squeeze of the tube, water is dispensed at the brush end.

Fill the waterbrush and squeeze out a drop onto the work surface. Dip the brush end in the drop of water and then apply it to the metal clay with the brush end. This intermediate step allows you to control the amount of water and also prevents the metal clay from clogging the brush.

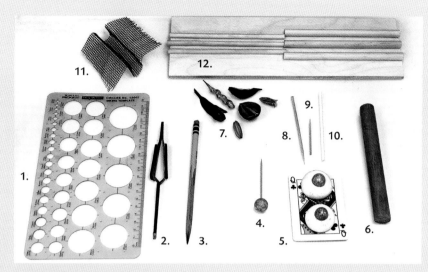

Supports and Template

1. plastic circle template **2.** crosslock tweezers **3.** pencil sanded as construction support for Tubular Bead #1 project **4.** stone bead and toothpick (construction support for Winged Hollow Bead project) **5.** stone beads and polymer clay (construction support in Tubular Bead #2 project) **6.** wooden dowel **7.** assorted natural pods for slip-painting **8.** skewer **9.** toothpick **10.** paper lollipop stick **11.** copper screening bent to support metal clay form while drying (for Vessel Bead project) **12.** dowel support (construction support for Draped Bead project)

Enameling and Stone-setting Tools

1. enamel scoop **2.** fine tweezers **3.** eyedropper **4.** extra-fine paintbrushes **5.** small enamel sifter (with coin for faster sifting) **6.** kiln tripod (to support enameled bead while firing it) **7.** spatula (for moving bead into and out a kiln) **8.** cabochon gemstones and bezel cups (for Vessel Bead project) **9.** bezel rocker (for stone setting) **10.** tray for holding enamels **11.** small containers for holding sifted enamels **12.** small, tabletop kiln for firing enamels

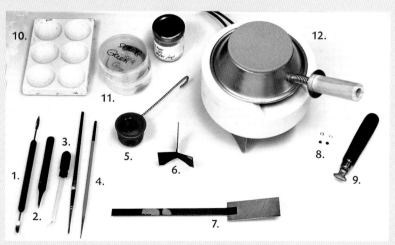

"Go out on a limb! That's where the fruit is!"
—Will Rogers

photo: Doug Foulkes Photography

Falling Water

ARTIST: Pat Gullett
MATERIALS: fine silver, freshwater pearl
TECHNIQUES: metal clay, hollow form constructions (Cork Clay core), patination, photopolymer plate texture
DIMENSIONS: 1¾" long × ¾" wide × ½" deep (45 mm × 20 mm × 13 mm)

Projects

The fifteen projects in this section are designed to take you on a trip from beginning to advanced metal clay techniques. Here are a few reminders to keep in mind as you work through the projects.

1. Metal clay can dry fairly quickly, depending on the dryness of the ambient air in your work area. To work efficiently, before you start, arrange all the materials and tools needed for the project on your worktable for ready access.

2. As you trim fresh metal clay from the project parts, return the trimmed pieces as soon as possible to the package with a bit of moist paper towel or wrap it in plastic wrap. Place the wrapped clay under a small overturned glass jar or juice glass with a small piece of moist paper towel.

3. Retrieve all sanding dust and dried bits of metal clay so you can combine them with water to make homemade slip.

4. A small mug warmer is a good tool for drying metal clay. When you're ready to remove dried metal clay parts from the heated mug warmer, move them with a pair of tweezers. Be careful—metal clay absorbs and transfers heat.

5. Work with a filled waterbrush or wet paintbrush to moisten dried metal clay parts that need to be joined.

6. When drilling through the dry metal clay to make the bead holes for some of the projects, choose a drill bit size that will accommodate the diameter of the stringing material you've decided to use.

7. All suggested measurements, other than any patterns, are approximate to allow you to make your own design decisions as you work.

8. Before you even open that package of metal clay, take the time to read through the entire project instructions. Then as you work, each step will seem familiar.

9. These projects are designed to guide you. If you decide, after you've gained some experience with metal clay, that you want to improvise, do it! Keep the concepts in mind, but alter the designs a little if you'd like (or a lot). Make the beads your own.

Disk
BEAD
with Appliquéd End Caps

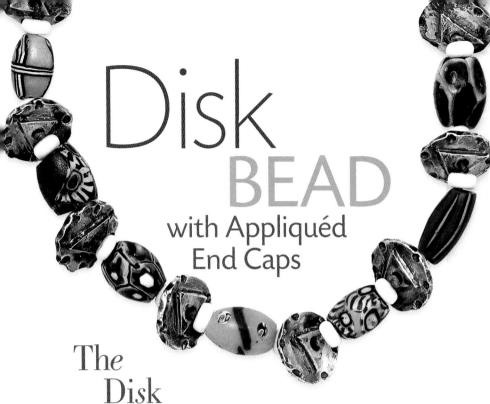

"Here's a simple, solid, and lovely bead to start with."

The Disk Bead

with Appliquéd End Caps is a simple, solid bead that you can adapt for a variety of uses. It can stand on its own as a focal bead or be used as a simple spacer bead, depending on its overall dimensions and the size of the other beads in the piece of jewelry. Although these project instructions and quantities are for a single disk bead, the finished necklace shown here incorporates thirteen equal-sized disk beads that I used as spacer beads between the other beads in the necklace. Another design variation might be to make a series of disk beads in graduated sizes to position between other types of beads.

The finished Disk Beads as spacer beads on necklace of antique trade beads, strung on hand-knotted silk.

"Make mistakes faster. Capture accidents." Bruce Mau

What You Will Need

- about 1.75 g of PMC Standard (also known as Original)
- 1 container of PMC3 slip
- 1 small bottle of olive oil (or other suitable lubricant)
- 1 piece of cellulose kitchen sponge, 1" (25 mm) square
- 1 porcelain or stainless-steel saucer or similar container (for the oiled sponge)
- 1 spatula or tissue blade
- 1 work surface (tempered glass or Plexiglas sheet)
- 1 plastic roller
- 1 brass clay cutter or short length of brass tubing, about ¾" (19 mm) in diameter
- 1 brass clay cutter or short length of brass tubing, about ⅛" (3 mm) in diameter
- 1 toothpick
- assorted salon boards or wet/dry emery paper in several grits
- 2 six-card stacks of playing cards
- 2 four-card stacks of playing cards
- 1 mug warmer
- 1 filled waterbrush (or small container of water and fine-tipped sable paintbrush)
- 1 color or clay shaper
- 1 art knife (X-Acto, for example)
- 1 PMC kiln
- 1 fireproof surface for the kiln with good, active ventilation
- 1 firing surface, kiln pad, or firebrick
- 1 pair long barbecue tongs
- 1 barbecue spatula
- 1 pair extra-heavy leather work gloves or potter's gloves (fire retardant)
- 1 large stainless-steel bowl filled with cool water
- 1 pair long steel tweezers

MAKING THE CENTER DISK

1. Lightly oil the spatula or the tissue blade (very carefully, after taping the dull edge of the blade—see the Tip at right). Lightly oil your hands, work surface, plastic roller, the brass cutters or tubing.

2. Break off one tip of the toothpick. With a salon board or emery paper, sand the broken end of the toothpick so it is relatively flat and then lightly oil it. Set the toothpick aside.

3. Place a lump of metal clay about ¼" (6 mm) in diameter on the work surface. Place one six-card stack of cards on either side of the metal clay. Use the roller to roll the metal clay into a sheet, level with the height of the cards.

4. Use the larger brass clay cutter or tubing to punch out a single disk of metal clay sheet **(A)**. Leaving the clay disk on the work surface, remove and wrap the excess clay and return it to the package or plastic wrap.

5. Create a scalloped pattern on the edge of both sides of the disk. Gently press the oiled end of the toothpick evenly around the edge of the circle in the following pattern, corresponding to positions on the face of an analog clock **(B)**.

6. Carefully lift the disk off the work surface and flip it over. Gently press the oiled end of the toothpick around the edge of the disk as you did in step 5, offsetting the impressions so they don't "erase" the impressions you made on the other side of the disk.

7. Use the smaller-diameter cutter or tube to cut a circle in the center of the metal clay disk. Lift the disk from the work surface with the tissue blade and set it aside to air-dry or dry on a mug warmer.

8. When the disk is completely dry, sand and refine its edges with salon boards or emery paper.

A. The center disk is cut from the metal clay sheet with a large circle cutter.

B. Toothpick impressions form the beginning of the scalloped pattern on the first side of the disk.

MAKING THE APPLIQUÉ END CAPS

1. Place a lump of metal clay about ¼" (6 mm) in diameter on the work surface. Place one four-card stack of cards on either side of the metal clay. Use the roller to roll the metal clay into a sheet, level with the height of the cards.

2. Use the smaller brass clay cutter or brass tubing to punch two holes in the sheet, about 1" (25 mm) apart.

3. Use the tissue blade to cut a triangular shape around each of the holes. Lift the triangles from the work surface with the tissue blade. Set the triangles aside to air-dry or dry on a mug warmer. Return the excess metal clay to the package or plastic wrap (C).

4. Check the triangular end caps every so often to make certain they are not warping. When the triangles are completely dry, sand and refine the edges with salon boards or emery paper.

C. The triangular end caps are cut from the sheet of metal clay with a tissue blade.

JOINING THE CENTER DISK AND THE APPLIQUÉ END CAPS

1. Working with the filled waterbrush or wet paintbrush, moisten the area around the center hole of the disk. Moisten one side of one of the appliqué end caps.

2. Scoop up some PMC3 slip with the shaper and apply the slip to the moistened side of the appliqué end cap. Use the tweezers to lift and hold the end cap steady while applying the slip.

3. Use the tweezers to place the appliqué end cap onto the center disk, pressing the end cap down with your finger and aligning the center holes. Don't worry if some of the slip oozes out into the hole. Rotate the appliqué end cap slightly, then realign it, securely joining it to the center disk (D).

4. Clean off the shaper by rolling it on the work surface or other smooth surface. Then use the shaper to clean the excess slip from the joints, wiping the slip off onto the work surface. Rotate the tool in the center hole to smooth the opening, removing any excess slip there. Use the slip to fill in any gaps in the joint. Return any excess slip to the slip container—or let it dry on the work surface and peel it off later to combine with homemade slip.

D. Join the end cap to the center disk by applying slip and pressing securely.

5. Repeat steps 1–4 to join the second appliqué end cap. Set the disk bead aside to air-dry or dry it on the mug warmer. When it is completely dry, carefully remove any excess slip with the tissue blade or art knife.

6. If the center hole is uneven, use a moistened shaper and/or toothpick to smooth its edges. Sand the edges and other surfaces until the bead is clean and smooth enough to be fired. If necessary, moisten rough areas and smooth using the shaper, then dry again.

FIRING THE DISK BEAD

1. Place the firing surface, kiln pad, or firebrick in a cold kiln.

2. Place the bead on the surface and close the kiln door.

3. Turn on the kiln and select the program that will allow the kiln to run for 2 hours at 1650°F (900°C).

4. After the kiln has completed the firing cycle, allow it to cool down a little. Then open the door to allow it to cool down even more.

5. Check the digital readout of the temperature on the kiln and, after the kiln has cooled down, put on the heavy gloves and move the bead with tweezers either to another fireproof surface to air-cool or into a large stainless-steel bowl filled with cool water to quench it.

6. Finish and polish bead (see page 25).

Tip

To smooth the edges and refine the joints of the bead, lightly moisten them and rub down with a shaper.

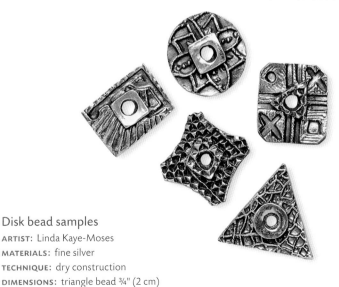

Disk bead samples
ARTIST: Linda Kaye-Moses
MATERIALS: fine silver
TECHNIQUE: dry construction
DIMENSIONS: triangle bead ¾" (2 cm)

Cube
BEAD

SKILL LEVEL: Beginner
FINISHED SIZE: ½" wide × ½" high × ³⁄₈" deep
(13 mm × 13 mm × 9 mm)

"The Cube Bead explores the use of design punches and stamps."

The **Cube Bead** provides an easy introduction to metal clay bead making. It's a solid bead embellished with a textured "belt." This project also introduces the use of design punches and stamps.

The measurements in this project are approximate. The bead, although it is cubelike, does not have to be an exact cube, with all sides and angles equal. Exact measurements, although useful in some designs, are not always essential. The construction of this project only requires that you get the concepts. The final design may in fact be more interesting if the measurements aren't exact. In other words, don't sweat the small stuff.

The finished Cube Bead as focal point on necklace of stones of lapis lazuli, strung on hand-knotted silk.

"The best time to plant a tree is twenty years ago; the next best time is now." Anonymous

What You Will Need

- about 6.5 g of PMC Standard (also known as Original)
- 1 container of PMC3 slip
- 1 small bottle of olive oil (or other suitable lubricant)
- 1 piece of cellulose kitchen sponge, 1" (25 mm) square
- 1 porcelain or stainless-steel saucer or similar container (for the oiled sponge)
- 1 work surface (tempered glass or Plexiglas)
- 1 tissue blade
- 1 paper lollipop stick
- 1 mug warmer
- 1 jeweler's or leather-design stamping punch or letterpress ornament
- 1 small ruler
- 1 plastic roller
- 2 four-card stacks of playing cards
- assorted salon boards or wet/dry emery paper in several grits
- 1 small hand mirror
- 1 sheet clean paper
- 1 small covered plastic or glass container
- 1 filled waterbrush (or small container of water and fine-tipped sable paintbrush)
- 1 color shaper or clay shaper
- 1 art knife (X-Acto, for example)
- 1 PMC kiln
- 1 fireproof surface for the kiln with good, active ventilation
- 1 firing surface, kiln pad, or firebrick
- 1 pair long barbecue tongs
- 1 barbecue spatula
- 1 pair extra-heavy leather work gloves or potter's gloves (fire retardant)
- 1 large stainless-steel bowl filled with cool water
- 1 pair long steel tweezers

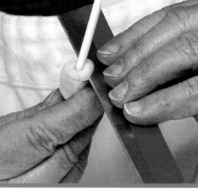

A. Form the squared lump of PMC clay around the stick.

B. Trim the squared lump around the stick with the tissue blade.

C. Dry the cube, on its lollipop stick, on the mug warmer until thoroughly dry.

MAKING THE CUBE

1. After taping the dull edge of the blade (for visibility), carefully and lightly lubricate the sharp edge and one-third of the stick with the olive oil and sponge.

2. Remove a lump of PMC Standard, about ¾" (19 mm) in diameter, from the package.

3. Wrap this lump around the paper lollipop stick until the shape is round.

4. Hold the paper stick and use the fingers of your other hand to press the sides of the metal clay, rotating the paper stick, until the clay becomes cubelike. Keep the sides about equal. The shaping may stretch the cube, loosening it a little. The form will be sanded to a more precise shape later in the project (**A**).

5. Use the tissue blade to trim and flatten the sides of the cube where the paper stick protrudes (**B**).

6. Set the cube, stick and all, on the mug warmer to dry (**C**). Because the cube is solid, it may take up to a few hours or even overnight to dry completely. When the cube is partially dry, you may be able to remove the lollipop stick from the hole. (If you can't, trim the stick close to the bead; any portion left in the hole will burn out with firing.)

MAKING THE BELT ELEMENTS

1. While the cube is drying, lightly oil your stamp or punch, the work surface, and the roller.

2. Roll a small lump of PMC Standard into a long cigar shape, about 1" long × ¼" around (25 mm long × 6 mm around). Place the clay on your work surface and flatten it slightly with your finger.

3. Place one four-card stack of playing cards on each side of the flattened lump on the work surface. With the roller, roll the lump into a long sheet level with height of the cards (**D**).

4. Lightly press the stamp or punch in a straight line along the length of the sheet of metal clay to produce a design (**E**). Don't press so hard that you pierce the metal clay sheet. (You can tell if you've pressed through the metal clay sheet by lifting your work surface and looking at the underside of the metal clay sheet. If it looks like you have pierced it, roll it up again and repeat from step 2 with the same lump of clay. You might have to add a drop of water to rehydrate the clay a little.)

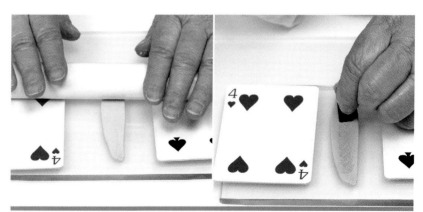

D. Roll out the metal clay into a long sheet, controlling the thickness with the two stacks of playing cards.

E. Lightly press the stamp or punch along the clay to produce the textured design.

5. Make two parallel cuts along the length of the sheet with the tissue blade, one on each side of the impressed design, to form a long strip of metal clay with the designs running the length of it.

6. Measure one side of your cube with the ruler. Cut two sections of the metal clay strip equal to that measurement. Cut two more sections of the metal clay strip equal to that measurement plus ⅛" (3 mm). You should now have two short and two slightly longer lengths cut from the strip (**F**).

   These will be joined, one at a time, to the sides of the cube to make a beltlike embellishment. Set the strips on the mug warmer to dry them completely, checking them occasionally for curving or warping. If they have developed curves, straighten them gently and place them back on the warmer. If they've dried completely and are warped, lightly moisten the smooth side and wait a minute for the water to be absorbed. Then test for pliability. If they are still too stiff, moisten a little more, check again. Flatten when they are pliable.

F. With the tissue blade, cut two short and two slightly longer lengths from the strip of clay.

Tip

To determine if the cube is fully dry, rest it on the surface of the mirror for about 30 seconds. If moisture condenses on the mirror, the cube is still not dry and should be returned to the warmer.

REFINING THE CUBE

1. When the cube is completely dry, lay it on a salon board or emery paper on top of a clean piece of paper. Beginning with the coarsest grit and progressing to finer grits, move the piece back and forth to sand all the sides until they are even, smooth, and flat. Place the small ruler alongside the cube from time to time, just to check that you are getting close to the final dimensions you want.

2. When you finish sanding the cube, set it aside. Pick up the paper with the sanding dust on it and deposit the dust into the small container. When you've collected enough, you can reconstitute the dust for slip.

3. When the four strips are dry, use salon boards to gently sand the edges and backs so that they are crisp and smooth.

JOINING THE CUBE AND THE BELT ELEMENTS

1. Use the filled waterbrush or wet paintbrush to apply a light "path" of water on one side of the cube, centered between the top and bottom of the cube (the sides where the paper stick protrudes).

2. Use the waterbrush or paintbrush to moisten the smooth underside of one of the two short dry metal clay strips.

3. Working with the color shaper or clay shaper, apply a layer of PMC3 slip on the moistened path on the cube.

4. Press the strip onto the slipped path on the cube, rotating back and forth to secure it. Don't worry about any excess slip that might ooze out right now. You will clean it up once it's dry (**G**).

5. Repeat from step 1 of this section for the second short metal clay strip, joining it to the opposite side of the cube. Set it aside to dry on the mug warmer.

G. Attach one of the short metal clay strips to the cube with a layer of slip. Press the strip to secure it.

I. Carefully remove excess slip with the art knife or X-Acto, moving the blade away from your fingers.

6. When the joint is completely dry, if necessary, gently sand the ends of each of the two strips so that they don't protrude past the corner of the cube.

7. Moisten a "path" of water on one of the remaining sides of the cube (across the ends of the two short strips) and on the smooth side of one of the longer metal clay strips, as in steps 1 and 2 of this section. Add slip to the moistened path on the cube.

8. Attach the moistened long strip to the slipped path on the cube. The ends of the long strip will protrude beyond the corner of the cube. You'll trim them later.

9. Repeat steps 7 and 8 of this section with the second long strip and the last side of the cube. Set the bead aside to dry completely **(H)**.

H. When you've attached all four metal clay strips, dry the cube completely.

REFINING THE CUBE BEAD

1. Remove or slice off any excess dried slip. Deposit the excess in the small container, with the dust, to be reconstituted as slip **(I)**.

2. Use the salon boards or emery paper to sand all the surfaces of the cube. If the holes are ragged, moisten the tip of the shaper and twirl it in the holes to refine them. (If you were not able to remove the paper stick in the hole, clean around it with the point of the scribe or a toothpick.)

3. Sand the ends of the longer metal clay strips until they are even with the surface of the shorter strips. Don't neglect the little edges—sand them flat. If you sand and smooth carefully now, you'll have less to do after firing the bead.

   Keep any sanding dust that contains paper fibers from the paper lollipop stick in a separate container. This dust cannot be used to make slip because the paper fibers would interfere with the sintering process. Instead, you can send this material to precious metal refiners for recycling (refiners set varying minimum amounts).

4. Check that all the joints are filled. Fill any gaps or cracks with slip (if they're narrow) or fresh PMC Standard (if they're wide). Dry again and then sand with increasingly finer grits of salon boards and/or emery paper.

Cube bead samples
ARTIST: Linda Kaye-Moses
MATERIALS: fine silver
TECHNIQUE: dry construction
DIMENSIONS:

FIRING THE CUBE BEAD

1. Place the firing surface, kiln pad, or firebrick into a cold kiln. Place the bead on it and close the kiln door.

2. Turn on the kiln and select the program that will allow the kiln to run for 2 hours at 1650°F (900°C).

3. After the kiln has completed the firing cycle, allow it to cool down a little and open the door to allow it to cool down even more.

4. Check the digital readout of the temperature on the kiln and, after the kiln has cooled down, using the tweezers and wearing the gloves, move the bead to either another fireproof surface to air-cool or quench it in a large stainless-steel bowl filled with cool water.

5. Finish and polish bead (see page 25).

Reversible
BEAD

SKILL LEVEL: Beginner
FINISHED SIZE: ⅝" × high by ¾" wide × ¼" deep
(16 mm × 20 mm × 6 mm)

"There are two sides to every story. Add texture to a reversible metal clay bead."

The Reversible Bead

project explores how to add texture to metal clay with rubber and metal stamps. Each side of this solid bead is decorated with an appliqué element. The holes for the bead are reinforced with the end caps.

You can make this bead from any metal clay product, but I suggest PMC Standard. This formula has a greater shrinkage rate than others, which enhances the textural interest. Also, because this bead is solid and requires more metal clay, PMC Standard is a more economical choice.

PMC Standard is less dense than the other formulas and, even though the bead is solid, it will be a little lighter than a solid bead of the same size made with PMC+ or PMC3. Weight is an important consideration when making a large bead like this one.

What You Will Need

- about 2.75 g of PMC Standard (also known as Original)
- 1 container of PMC3 slip
- 1 small bottle of olive oil (or other suitable lubricant)
- 1 piece of cellulose kitchen sponge, 1" (25 mm) square
- 1 porcelain or stainless-steel saucer or similar container (for the oiled sponge)
- 1 tissue blade
- 1 work surface (tempered glass or Plexiglas)
- 1 piece of Plexiglas sheet or other smooth, flat plastic object, approximately 3" (7.5 cm) square
- 2 different rubber stamps with a relatively deep texture or image
- 1 filled waterbrush (or small container of water and fine-tipped sable paintbrush)
- 1 skewer or a paper lollipop stick
- plastic wrap
- 1 pair fine-tip tweezers (such as soldering tweezers)
- 1 pair long steel tweezers
- assorted salon boards or wet/dry emery paper in several grits
- 1 color shaper or clay shaper
- 1 mug warmer or hair dryer
- 1 plastic roller
- 1 jeweler's or leather-design stamping punch or letterpress ornament
- 2 four-card stacks of playing cards

The finished Reversible Bead, centered on necklace of amethyst rondelles, strung on hand-knotted silk.

"Do, or do not. There is no 'try.'" Yoda, **The Empire Strikes Back**

A. Place the clay on a textured stamp and press to transfer the textured design.

B. Press a skewer or lollipop stick into the first side of the bead to form a hole of the desired diameter.

MAKING THE FIRST SIDE OF THE BEAD BODY

1. After taping the dull edge of the tissue blade (for visibility), carefully and lightly lubricate the sharp edge and then your hands with the olive oil and the sponge. Lubricate the work surface, Plexiglas sheet, rubber stamps, and the textures you intend to use. Fill the waterbrush, or small container, with water.

- 1 brass clay cutter or short length of brass tubing, ⅛" to ³⁄₁₆" (3 to 5 mm) in diameter. The tubing should fit around skewer or lollipop stick.
- 2 five-card stacks of playing cards
- 1 pair side cutters
- 1 art knife (X-Acto, for example)
- 1 PMC kiln
- 1 fireproof surface for the kiln and good, active ventilation
- 1 firing surface, kiln pad, or firebrick
- 1 pair long barbecue tongs
- 1 barbecue spatula
- 1 pair extra-heavy leather work gloves or potter's gloves (fire retardant)
- 1 large stainless-steel bowl filled with cool water

2. Take out a lump of PMC about 1" (2.5 cm) in diameter. Put the remainder of the metal clay back in its wrapping and seal it in the original package.

3. Working with the oiled tissue blade, divide the lump of metal clay into two pieces, one slightly smaller than the other, but about ⅝" (16 mm) in diameter. Each section will make one side of the bead. Tightly reseal the remaining clay in plastic wrap and set it aside.

4. Roll the smaller piece of clay between your hands until it is relatively round.

5. Place one of your oiled rubber stamps on the work surface.

6. With the palm of your hand, press the round piece of PMC on top of the stamp, flattening the clay slightly but not thinning it excessively.

7. Place the Plexiglas sheet on top and gently flatten the metal clay. Press only hard enough to achieve an even surface and a good texture **(A)**. Lift the stamp–metal clay–Plexiglas "sandwich" to check the thickness. The clay should be about ⅛" (3 mm) thick. If the clay looks too thin, roll it up and repeat steps 5–7.
    Keep in mind that the PMC will shrink 28 percent during the firing process, so visualize your finished piece

as being that much smaller. If it doesn't look like it will be the correct finished size, add or subtract a little clay now and repeat steps 4–7.

8. Remember, the finished bead will be metal and should be a comfortable size and weight to wear. (As you become more familiar with metal clay, estimating size and weight will become easier and more instinctive.)

9. Leaving the metal clay on the rubber stamp, lift or slide the Plexiglas sheet off the metal clay. To remove the Plexiglas easily, slide it sideways, rather than trying to lift it straight up.

MAKING THE SECOND SIDE OF THE BEAD BODY

1. Use the shaper to paint PMC3 slip all over the surface of the clay.

2. Press the skewer into the slip-covered surface across the diameter or center of the metal clay, so that about half the thickness of the skewer remains above the surface. This depression will become the hole for the bead **(B)**. Do not remove the clay from the rubber stamp, but cover the entire assembly lightly with plastic wrap.

C. Center the second half of the bead over the first half and gently press it in place.

D. The slip on the surfaces of the two halves holds them in place to form the bead body.

E. Work carefully with the tissue blade to square the edges of the bead.

3. Lightly oil the second rubber stamp.

4. Remove the reserved lump of PMC from the plastic wrap and roll it between your oiled hands until it is nearly round. This piece will form the second half of your bead body.

5. With your finger, gently press the clay on top of the first piece and skewer, keeping it centered (**C**).

6. Press the rubber stamp on the surface of the second half. Use the Plexiglas sheet to firmly press the rubber stamp on the second half of the bead body, flattening it but not thinning it too much (**D**). The slip on the surfaces of the two sections will act as a glue to hold them together around the skewer.

7. Remove the upper rubber stamp and lift the bead off the lower rubber stamp. Moving the sharp tissue blade in a direction away from your fingers, trim the edges of the bead so it is as square as possible (**E**). Wrap the trimmings in plastic wrap.

8. Dry the bead body completely on the mug warmer. Then remove the hot bead from the mug warmer with a pair of fine-tip tweezers. Allow the bead to cool, then sand and refine the edges with salon boards of various grits. If necessary, moisten and smooth the stubborn areas, including the area around the hole, with a shaper.

9. While the bead body dries, check that the joints are filled and, if needed, add slip or fresh PMC and dry again. You can sand and refine these joints later.

F. Dry the decorated appliqué elements and bead body on the mug warmer.

MAKING THE APPLIQUÉ ELEMENTS

1. While the bead body is drying, lubricate the work surface, the roller, and the punch or ornament.

2. Roll a small lump of PMC into a ball about ¼" (6 mm) in diameter. Place the ball on your work surface and flatten it slightly with your finger.

3. Place a four-card stack of cards on either side of the flattened lump. With the roller, roll the lump into a sheet, level with the height of the cards.

4. Gently press the punch or ornament onto the clay sheet to form a design. Reposition the punch or ornament about 1" (25 mm) away from the first pressing and press again.

5. Trim around the designs in the sheet to make individual appliqué elements. You can trim them into the shape of a square, circle, or triangle (or any other shape you want) using a tissue blade, brass tubing, or circle cutters.

6. Remove each appliqué element from the work surface by slipping the tissue blade under the edges of the element, and then rotating the blade to lift each side. Then lift the entire element.

7. Dry the elements completely, checking to make sure they dry flat (**F**). If the appliqué elements have warped slightly, wet the untextured sides slightly with the waterbrush and wait for the water to be absorbed. Check the elements again to see if they are pliable—if so, gently press them flat to dry.

8. When the appliqué elements are completely dry, sand and refine all their surfaces and edges with salon boards or emery paper.

MAKING THE END CAPS

1. While the body and appliqué elements dry, roll out a sheet of five-card-thick PMC on the lubricated work surface.

2. Using the brass tubing, punch two holes in the sheet, at least ½" (13 mm) apart.

3. Moving the tissue blade away from your fingers, trim each end cap into a small square centered around each hole. Set aside to dry.

4. When the end caps are dry, sand and refine all the edges with salon boards or emery paper.

JOINING THE BODY, APPLIQUÉ ELEMENTS, AND END CAPS

1. With the filled waterbrush or wet paintbrush, lightly moisten the untextured side of one of the appliqué elements and the center of the bead body.

2. Press the moistened appliqué element onto the moistened center of the body half, rotating the pieces slightly and then realigning them to adjust the placement and join securely.

3. Repeat steps 1 and 2 for the second appliqué element.

4. With the waterbrush or paintbrush, wet the area around the skewer on one end of the bead body and add a little slip. Wet one side of one of the end caps.

5. Slip the moistened end cap over the skewer and press gently into the slip, rotating and adjusting the placement to join securely.

6. Repeat steps 4 and 5 for the second end cap.

7. Set the pieces aside to dry thoroughly (**G**). When the bead is almost dry, you might be able to remove the skewer. If you can't, leave the skewer in place. When the pieces are completely dry, add slip where needed to refine joints.

8. If you've left the skewer in place, clip the excess with the side cutter. Sand and refine around the hole.

9. Keeping your fingers away from the blade, remove any excess slip with the art knife. Deposit the excess into a container to rehydrate as slip.

G. Join and dry all the refined and dried parts of the bead (bead body, appliqué elements, and end caps).

FIRING THE REVERSIBLE BEAD

1. Place the firing surface, kiln pad, or firebrick in a cold kiln.

2. Place the bead on top of the surface and close the kiln door.

3. Turn on the kiln and select the program that will allow the kiln to run for 2 hours at 1650°F (900°C).

4. After the kiln has completed the firing cycle, allow it to cool down a little. Then open the door to allow it to cool down even more.

5. Check the digital readout of the temperature on the kiln and, after the kiln has cooled down, put on the heavy gloves and move the bead with long tweezers either to another fireproof surface to air-cool or into a large stainless-steel bowl filled with cool water.

6. Finish and polish bead (see page 25).

Slip-Painted BEAD

"With slip-painting, you can replicate pods, twigs, and leaves."

Slip-painting

is the building up of PMC slip in layers. You can coat and replicate the shape of almost any small three-dimensional object or model that you want to reproduce without making a mold—pods, twigs, and thick leaves, to name a few. Hollow objects, like the pod I've used for this project, are especially wonderful.

There are three stipulations for choosing the object. It must be completely dry. It must be a material that will burn out in the kiln, but should not include solid wood, which can raise the temperature in the bead and melt it. It should not release toxic fumes when burned, so avoid Styrofoam, plastic, polymer clay models.

Before you begin, review the steps for working with slip in the sidebar on page 48.

The finished Slip-Painted Bead with freshwater pearls, strung on hand-knotted silk.

"So you see, imagination needs moodling, long, inefficient happy idling, dawdling and puttering." Brenda Ueland

What You Will Need

- 1 partial package of PMC3 (about 1 gram)
- about 5 g of PMC3 slip
- white glue
- 1 skewer, toothpick, or paper lollipop stick
- 1 small botanical specimen to serve as a model
- 1 color or clay shaper
- 1 work surface (tempered glass or Plexiglas)
- 1 clean, small to medium-size sable paintbrush
- 1 small square of Styrofoam
- 1 pair cross-lock tweezers (optional)
- plastic wrap
- 1 mug warmer or hair dryer
- 1 small plastic container (such as a yogurt container)
- 1 small bottle of olive oil (or other suitable lubricant)
- 1 piece of cellulose kitchen sponge, 1" (25 mm) square

- 1 porcelain or stainless-steel saucer or similar container (for the oiled sponge)
- 1 tissue blade
- 1 plastic roller
- 1 brass clay cutter or short length of brass tubing, about ⅛" (3 mm) in diameter
- 1 brass clay cutter or short length of brass tubing, about ⅜" (10 mm) in diameter
- 2 three-card stacks of playing cards
- 1 needle tool or scribe
- 1 pair side cutters
- assorted salon boards, coarse and fine
- 1 art knife (X-Acto, for example)
- 1 PMC kiln
- 1 fireproof surface for the kiln with good, active ventilation

A. A paper lollipop stick provides a handle with which to hold the pod.

B. Coat the entire surface of the model with slip.

C. A secure support will allow the slip to dry without marring the surfaces of the painted model.

SLIP-PAINTING THE MODEL

- 1 Kaowool insulated firing pad, 6" (15 cm) square
- 1 firing surface, kiln pad, or firebrick
- 1 pair long barbecue tongs
- 1 barbecue spatula
- 1 pair extra-heavy leather work gloves or potter's gloves (fire retardant)
- 1 large stainless-steel bowl filled with cool water
- 1 pair long steel tweezers

1. Place a dab of white glue on one end of the skewer, toothpick, or lollipop stick. Press the glued end into the model at the spot where you want to position the hole for the bead. Allow the glue to dry completely. The "handle" allows you to hold the model while you paint it with slip **(A)**.

2. With the shaper, scoop a small amount of PMC3 slip onto the work surface. Add one or two drops of water to the slip. Use the shaper to stir the water into the slip until the water has been absorbed and the slip is smooth.

3. Hold the model by the handle and, with your paintbrush, paint the model with a layer of slip **(B)**. Coat the entire surface.

4. To support the model while it dries, press the stick into the Styrofoam square **(C)**. Or, clasp the handle in a pair of cross-lock tweezers. Either

Hollow pods are especially well suited as models for slip-painting.

method will allow the bead to dry without disturbing the slip and will leave your hands free to use a hair dryer to speed the drying. When the slip is partially dry, you can set the model on a mug warmer to dry completely.

5. While the slip is drying, cover the remaining diluted slip with plastic wrap. To prevent the paintbrush bristles from hardening between applications of slip, scrape the brush against the edge of the slip jar. Then place the brush in a plastic container of water (covering only the bristles). When ready to apply the next layer of slip, just wipe the brush lightly on a paper towel.

6. Continue to add layers of slip, drying thoroughly between layers, until there are at least 10 to 12 layers of slip. You can use undiluted slip, straight from the jar, after the first layer or two. Set the model aside to dry between layers. (See the sidebar on page 48 for tips on measuring the thickness of the layers of slip.)

7. Leave the slip-painted model on the mug warmer for 5 to 10 minutes to make certain that it's completely dry.

Working with Slip

Slip is thinned with a little water for slip-painting. I don't add water to the entire jar of slip for two reasons: I'll probably want to use the rest of the slip for other processes, and I'll only need a small amount of thinned slip for the first and possibly second layers. (If you are coating a very thin or fragile object, such as a leaf, however, you'll want to apply several thin layers.)

To thin slip, stir the jar of slip with a color or clay shaper. Scoop a little slip (about ¼ teaspoon) from the jar and place it on your work surface. Add a tiny drop of water and stir with the shaper until the slip is smooth and a little thinner than what came out of the jar (you might have to add a little more water). Thinned slip should have a consistency somewhere between a thick nail polish and white glue. If the slip is too thin, just leave it exposed to the air for a few minutes and it will be ready to use.

Choose a relatively small watercolor or oil paintbrush, preferably with sable hairs, to evenly apply the slip to all surfaces of the object. I like to use a brush that has good quality short bristles and is a little stiff.

You'll want to check the thickness of the layers as you paint—without having to cut into the piece to check! Before you begin, measure the diameter of the object with calipers. After painting several layers, measure the diameter again. A good thickness would be three to five playing cards thick (compare the caliper measurements to the card thicknesses). When slip-painting beads, you can also get a good view of the thickness of the layers by checking the area around the hole in the bead.

MAKING THE HOLE SUPPORTS

1. After taping the dull edge of the tissue blade for visibility, carefully and lightly lubricate the sharp edge and then your hands with the olive oil and the sponge. Lubricate the work surface, the roller, the ⅛" (3 mm) -diameter clay cutter or brass tubing, and the ⅜" (10 mm) -diameter clay cutter or brass tubing.

2. Roll a small lump of PMC into a ball about ¼" (6 mm) in diameter. Place it on your work surface and flatten it slightly with your finger.

3. Place a three-card stack of playing cards on either side of the flattened lump and, using the plastic roller, roll the lump into a sheet, level with height of the cards.

4. With the ⅛" (3 mm)-diameter clay cutter or tubing, punch two holes in the metal clay sheet, no less than 1" (25 mm) apart. Do not remove the sheet from the work surface.

5. Cut one circle in the sheet, centered on the small hole, with the ⅜" (10 mm) -diameter clay cutter or tubing, to make a flattened doughnut shape.

6. Working carefully with the tissue blade, lift away the excess metal clay sheet (in other words, everything except the doughnut). Lift out the metal clay from the small hole with the needle tool or scribe; remove and wrap the excess clay and return it to the package or plastic wrap.

7. Next, carefully lift the hole supports off the work surface with the tissue blade. Set the supports aside to air-dry or dry them on the mug warmer **(D)**.

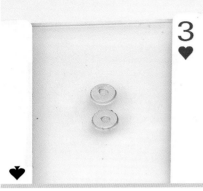

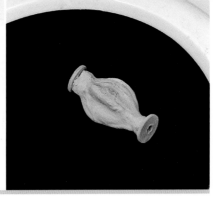

D. Allow the flattened hole supports to dry thoroughly. Hole supports do exactly what their name suggests—they support and reinforce the area around the hole in the bead so that whatever the bead is strung on, or next to, doesn't abrade that area.

E. Thoroughly dry the joined hole supports and the slip-painted model.

JOINING THE MODEL AND HOLE SUPPORTS

1. Sand the end of the slip-painted model opposite the handle so that it is flat. You should be able to see a little of the original model surrounded by the "skin" of the dried slip. (Remember, the dust from this sanding cannot be reconstituted as slip, because it contains dust from the model. Save it to send to a refiner.) Gently sand the edges of the dry hole supports. These parts are fragile and somewhat brittle in this state, so sand very gently.

2. Hold the slip-painted model by the handle, moisten the end opposite the handle, and then add a dab of PMC3 slip to the moistened spot.

3. Moisten one side of one hole support and place that side on the dab of slip. Rotate the support a little, pressing gently at the same time to secure the joint. Twirl a shaper in the hole to clear away any excess slip. Dry completely with the hair dryer or mug warmer.

4. With side cutters, carefully trim the handle as close to the model's surface

as possible. Be careful not to apply any downward pressure. If the handle still protrudes, gently sand it with a coarse salon board so it is flush with the surface of the model.

5. Lightly moisten the area around the hole and add a dab of PMC3 slip to the spot. Lightly moisten one side of the remaining hole support and press that side gently onto the dab of slip. Rotate the support a little to make it secure and realign it. Clear out the hole with a shaper and dry it completely with the hair dryer or mug warmer **(E)**.

6. When the bead is completely dry, remove any excess dried slip around the joints with the art knife. Sand and refine any unwanted irregularities on the surfaces with salon boards. Smooth any flaws with a moistened shaper and fill any gaps in the joints with fresh slip. Dry completely and then refine the joints again.

Organic Rounds

ARTIST: Terry Kovalcik
MATERIALS: fine silver
TECHNIQUES: PMC3 paste, hollow core construction, painting, patination
DIMENSIONS: 5/16" to 3/4" (8 mm to 19 mm)

FIRING THE BEAD

1. Place the Kaowool firing pad on the firing surface, kiln pad, or firebrick in a cold kiln. Because this bead is hollow, it requires the support of this special firing pad.

2. Place the bead on the firing pad and close the kiln door.

3. Turn on the kiln and select the program that will allow the kiln to run for 2 hours at 1650°F (900°C). Although PMC3 and PMC3 slip can be fired at lower temperatures, firing at this temperature and for this length of time produces a stronger bead.

4. After the kiln has completed the firing cycle, allow it to cool down a little. Then open the door to allow it to cool down even more.

5. Check the digital readout of the temperature on the kiln and, after the kiln has cooled down, put on the heavy gloves and move the bead with tweezers either to another fireproof surface to air-cool or into a large stainless-steel bowl filled with cool water to quench it.

5. Finish and polish bead (see page 25).

photo: Corrin Jacobsen Kovalcik

Tubular
BEAD #1

SKILL LEVEL: Beginner to intermediate
FINISHED SIZE: 3/8" diameter × 1" high
(10 mm × 25 mm)

> "The Tubular Bead #1
> is a bead of
> infinite variety."

Tubular Bead #1

is a hand-wrapped bead. It is textured with a rubber stamp, and the holes are literally hand-drilled with a small drill bit so that the bead will hang vertically. This bead can be designed in many possible ways. It can be hung vertically (as in this project) or horizontally. It can be duplicated in matching or graduated sizes. It can be suspended like a pendant or made in multiples to string as a collar-type neckpiece.

To wrap the metal clay so it doesn't dry too quickly and crack, you'll paint it with a small amount of glycerin. This is the only bead project in the book that *must not be dried using a mug warmer, a hair dryer, or any other high-heat drying method.* If heated, it would give off smoke and make the metal clay unusable.

What You Will Need

- about 12 g of PMC3
- 1 container of PMC3 slip
- 1 transparency sheet
- pattern (figure 1, page 51)
- 1 permanent fine-line black marker
- 1 pair scissors
- 1 wooden pencil
- plastic wrap
- 1 work surface (tempered glass or Plexiglas)
- 1 rubber stamp sheet with a shallow, allover pattern or texture
- 1 plastic roller
- 1 small bottle of olive oil (or other suitable lubricant)
- 1 piece of cellulose kitchen sponge, 1" (25 mm) square
- 1 porcelain or stainless-steel saucer or similar container (for the oiled sponge)
- 1 tissue blade
- 2 four-card stacks of playing cards
- 2 three-card stacks of playing cards
- 1 color shaper or clay shaper
- 1 small jar of glycerin
- 1 brass clay cutter or short length of brass tubing, about 5/8" (16 mm) in diameter
- 1 mug warmer or hair dryer
- assorted salon boards or wet/dry emery paper in several grits
- 1 waterbrush (or small container of water and fine-tipped sable paintbrush)

The finished Tubular Bead #1 strung with tumbled quartz crystals on hand-knotted silk.

"It's okay if I don't think like everyone else! Go, Brain, Go!"
Qualcomm commercial

A. The stacks of playing cards act as a guide to help you roll the metal clay sheet to just the right thickness.

TRACING THE PATTERN

1. Place the transparency sheet over the pattern in figure 1 below. You'll transfer the pattern to the transparency to ensure that your pattern will be usable even if it gets oily or wet.

2. Trace the outline of the pattern exactly with the permanent marker. The proportions of this pattern will give you the correct dimensions for the bead.

3. Cut out the transparent tracing.

MAKING THE WRAPPED TUBE

1. After taping the dull edge of the tissue blade for visibility, carefully and lightly lubricate the sharp edge and then your hands with the olive oil and the sponge. Lightly oil the rubber stamp sheet, the work surface, and the roller.

2. Wrap the pencil in a single layer of plastic wrap and lightly oil the plastic wrap.

3. Take out a lump of PMC3 about 1" (25 mm) in diameter. Return the rest of the clay to the package or wrap with plastic wrap. Roll the clay into a sphere between your hands and press it lightly on the work surface.

4. Place one four-card stack of playing cards on each side of the flattened lump. With the roller, roll the lump into a sheet, level with height of the cards.

5. Working with the tissue blade, lift the metal clay sheet off the work surface and lay it on the rubber stamp sheet.

6. Use extra card stacks to raise the card stacks so that they are just three cards above the surface of the rubber stamp. With the roller, roll the metal clay onto the rubber stamp, level with height of the cards (**A**).

- 1 art knife (X-Acto, for example)
- 1 steel drill bit, size #46–50 (with pin vise to hold drill bit, optional)
- Tri-M-Ite polishing papers
- 1 PMC kiln
- 1 fireproof surface for the kiln with good, active ventilation
- 1 Kaowool insulated firing pad, 6" (15 cm) square
- 1 firing surface, kiln pad, or firebrick
- 1 pair long barbecue tongs
- 1 barbecue spatula
- 1 pair extra-heavy leather work gloves or potter's gloves (fire retardant)
- 1 large stainless-steel bowl filled with cool water
- 1 pair long steel tweezers

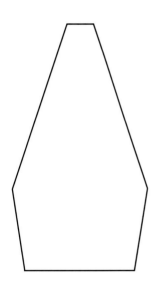

Figure 1: Bead Pattern (actual size)

B. Follow the traced outline of the pattern to cut the metal clay to shape.

C. Spread a very small amount of glycerin on the untextured surface of the metal clay sheet and let it soak in.

D. The metal clay is shaped by wrapping it around a plastic-wrapped pencil.

7. Again working carefully with the tissue blade, lift the metal clay sheet off the rubber stamp. Lay it, textured side down, on the work surface.

8. Place the transparent pattern on top of the untextured side of the metal clay. Keeping your fingers clear of the blade, cut the metal clay sheet to match the shape of the pattern **(B)**. Return the excess metal clay to the package and seal the package. Set aside the pattern.

9. Carefully lift and move the metal clay sheet to the mug warmer for no more than 15 seconds. Then return it to the work surface, textured side down.

10. With a clean shaper or your fingertip, add one very small spot of glycerin to the untextured side of the trimmed metal clay sheet. Use as little as you can. Spread the glycerin across the surface of the clay with your finger **(C)**. Let the glycerin absorb into the metal clay sheet for about 3 minutes.

11. Use a clean shaper to spread an even, thin layer of PMC3 slip on the untextured side of the sheet.

12. Working carefully with the tissue blade, lift the metal clay sheet off the work surface. Roll the clay around the plastic-wrapped pencil, positioning the wide base of the triangle-shaped pattern near the sharpened end. Don't roll it very tightly—just let it conform to the shape **(D)**.

13. After you've rolled the metal clay completely onto the pencil, gently rotate the pencil and bead in your hands to secure the joint. Don't press too hard, or the metal clay will stretch and lose its shape and texture. Hold the clay in place on the pencil for about 3 minutes to give the still-wet tube time to retain the shape. You cannot heat-dry this bead, but you can partially dry it with a hair dryer—very, very briefly—just enough so the bead retains its tubular shape.

(Drying may take a little longer than usual because of the glycerin.) The tube has fairly heavy walls and the weight may cause the shape to become distorted, separate, unroll, or change shape, so check it from time to time as it dries and gently reshape it, adding more slip if needed. To avoid compression, build "legs" of playing cards to support each end of the pencil as the beads dries.

14. When the tube is completely dry, slide it off the pencil by gently pulling the plastic wrap. Then sand and refine each end with salon boards or emery paper in several grits. Check to make sure that the roll is securely joined. Add slip if needed and let dry again.

15. Moisten the inside of the wrapped tube, near the opening, and refine and smooth the insides with a shaper. Sand the ends so the design is balanced.

E. The curve of the square hole supports should conform to the curve of the plastic-wrapped pencil.

F. A small amount of PMC3 slip and a little firm pressure secures the hole supports to the surface of the wrapped metal clay tube.

Tubular bead samples

ARTIST: Linda Kaye-Moses
MATERIALS: fine silver
TECHNIQUES: wrapped, coiled, dry construction
DIMENSIONS: ½" to 1" long (12 mm to 25 mm)

MAKING THE HOLE SUPPORTS

1. Wrap the pencil in many layers of plastic wrap so that the diameter is equal to the outside diameter of the metal clay tube.

2. Remove a lump of PMC3 from the package, about ¼" (6 mm) in diameter. Return the rest of the metal clay to the package or wrap in plastic. Place the lump in the center of the work surface and flatten it slightly.

3. Place one three-card stack of playing cards on each side of the flattened lump and roll the lump into a sheet, level with height of the cards.

4. Working carefully with the tissue blade, cut out two small, squarish shapes.

5. With the tissue blade, lift the squares off the work surface and drape them on the side of the wrapped pencil **(E)**. While the squares are still pliable but not soft, check the curve against the curve of the tube—they should match. Adjust the curves as needed.

6. Let the squares rest on the wrapped pencil until they are completely dry.

JOINING THE HOLE SUPPORTS AND TUBE

1. Lift the dried hole supports off the wrapped pencil and refine the edges with assorted salon boards or emery paper in several grits.

2. Check the wrapped tube for any repairs that may be needed. If the tube seems to be too flexible or fragile, reinsert the pencil for support. The pencil may not fit into the tube, however, because water in the metal clay has evaporated and the inside diameter of the tube may now be a little smaller than it was. Sand the pencil a little with a piece of coarse sandpaper. Then lubricate it with olive oil (just to be safe) before inserting it into the metal clay tube.

3. Moisten the inside curve of the hole supports with the filled waterbrush or a wet paintbrush. Moisten a spot on the outside of the wrapped tube, about ¼" (6 mm) away from one of the ends.

4. Working with a shaper, apply an even, small amount of PMC3 slip to the inside curve of one of the hole supports. Press the support onto the moistened spot on the wrapped tube. Rotate the support a little to firm up the joint and then readjust the position so it rests neatly on the side of the tube. There should be enough slip to have filled all gaps in the joint, including those depressions left by the texture of the rubber stamp.

5. Repeat steps 3 and 4, to secure the remaining support to the opposite side of the wrapped tube **(F)**.

6. Set the wrapped tube aside to air-dry. When it's completely dry, pop off any excess slip with the art knife. You can reconstitute this dried slip with water to make homemade slip. Sand and refine all the parts with salon boards or emery paper in several grits.

DRILLING THE HOLE SUPPORTS AND BEAD

1. The pencil will support the wrapped tube while you drill the bead's hole. Because the metal clay tube's opening has dried and shrunk somewhat, sand the pencil slightly (if you haven't already done this) and lubricate it with olive oil (for easy removal of the bead) before reinserting it into the wrapped tube.

2. Rest the bead on a clean work surface, with one support facing up. Make a pencil mark in the center of the support.

3. Stabilize the bead with one hand and rest the point of the drill bit on the pencil mark.

4. Without pressing too hard, rotate the drill bit, cutting into the surface of the support (**G**). As you rotate the bit, you are removing small curved pieces of dried metal clay from the hole support. You can add these pieces and any sanding dust to homemade slip.

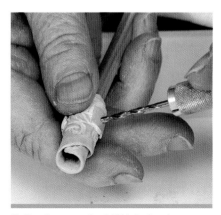

G. Gently rotate the drill bit by hand to cut into the surface of the hole support. Be careful not to exert too much pressure, or the fragile bead may break.

Tip

Work with Tri-M-Ite polishing papers just as you would emery paper or salon boards. Begin sanding with the coarsest grit and end with the finest grit. These abrasive papers are coated with extremely fine (micron-graded) grits and will create a very smooth surface.

5. Carefully drill through the support and wrapped tube, allowing the drill bit to do its job, without putting too much pressure on it. In this greenware (unfired) state, your bead is somewhat fragile, and too much pressure could crack it.

6. When the drill bit has broken through to the interior of the wrapped tube, you'll hit the pencil. Repeat steps 1–5 for the second hole support.

7. If the holes have any ragged edges, smooth the edges by twirling a moistened shaper in the holes. Check for any flaws or cracks and repair them with slip.

8. Sand with salon boards or emery papers to smooth and refine the bead. Use the Tri-M-Ite polishing papers to give the surfaces of the bead a more finished look before firing.

9. Set the bead aside to dry completely.

FIRING TUBULAR BEAD #1

1. Place the Kaowool firing pad on the firing surface, kiln pad, or firebrick in a cold kiln.

2. Place the bead on the firing pad and close the kiln door.

3. Turn on the kiln and select the program that will allow the kiln to run for 2 hours at 1650°F (900°C). Although PMC3 can be fired at lower temperatures, firing at this temperature and for this length of time produces a stronger bead.

4. After the kiln has completed the firing cycle, allow it to cool down a little. Open the door to allow it to cool down even more.

5. Check the digital readout of the temperature on the kiln and, after the kiln has cooled down, put on the heavy gloves and move the bead with tweezers either to another fireproof surface to air-cool or into a large stainless-steel bowl filled with cool water to quench it.

6. Finish and polish bead (see page 25).

Concentric Nitric

ARTIST: Catherine Davies Paetz

MATERIALS: fine and sterling silver, enamel

TECHNIQUES: metal clay; water etching with wax resist; enameling (wet-packed); construction over burnable core (lollipop stick); Viking knit chain

DIMENSIONS: ¾" wide × ⅜" diameter (2 cm × 1 cm)

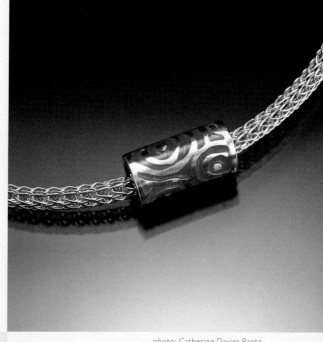

photo: Catherine Davies Paetz

photo: Barbara Briggs

Cylinder Beads Necklace

ARTIST: Barbara Briggs

MATERIALS: fine and sterling silver

TECHNIQUES: pressed designs, PMC+, tumbled, patination, polishing

DIMENSIONS: ⅜" (1 cm) average length

Mold-Formed BEAD

SKILL LEVEL: Intermediate
FINISHED SIZE: 1¹⁄₁₆" high × ½" wide × ½" deep
(26 mm × 13 mm × 13 mm)

"Add three-dimensional imagery."

With a mold

and a model, you can create decorative three-dimensional metal clay forms. I've chosen a small shell as my model. You can also choose fancy buttons, small ceramic knickknacks or miniature doll faces, old jewelry parts, or similar objects. To make the mold, you'll work with a two-part silicone material. (I used Belicold. See page 147 for more information about this mold-making material and others.)

Hole supports reinforce and strengthen the areas of a bead that are most stressed when the bead is strung. This bead is quite strong without the additional protection, but the supports give it a nice finished look.

The finished Mold-Formed Bead as focal point on strand of teardrop-shaped citrine beads.

"If you do not expect the unexpected, you will not find it." Wendell Castle

What You Will Need

- 6–7 g of PMC Standard (also known as Original)
- 1 container of PMC3 slip
- 1 set of two-part silicone mold-making material (such as Belicold)
- 1 decorative element or model
- 1 single plastic-coated playing card
- 1 small bottle of olive oil (or other suitable lubricant)
- 1 piece of cellulose kitchen sponge, 1" (25 mm) square
- 1 porcelain or stainless-steel saucer or similar container (for the oiled sponge)
- 1 work surface (tempered glass or Plexiglas)
- 1 tissue blade
- 1 skewer
- 1 brass clay cutter or short length of brass tubing that will fit over the skewer
- 1 round needle file
- 1 art knife (X-Acto, for example)
- 1 brass clay cutter or short length of brass tubing, about ⅛" (3 mm) larger in diameter than the clay cutter or brass tubing above
- 1 scribe
- 1 brass clay cutter or short length of brass tubing, about ⅛" (3 mm) in diameter
- 1 brass clay cutter or short length of brass tubing, with an outer diameter of ½" to ⅝" (13 mm to 16 mm)
- 1 clean work surface
- 1 mug warmer or hair dryer
- 1 paper clip, with one bent leg (or an art knife)
- 2 three-card stacks of playing cards
- 1 plastic roller
- 1 pencil
- 1 filled waterbrush (or small container of water and fine-tipped sable paintbrush)
- assorted salon boards or wet/dry emery paper in several grits

A. Remove the model from the cured and hardened mold.

- 1 small color or clay shaper
- 1 pair small, fine-pointed tweezers
- 1 PMC kiln
- 1 fireproof surface for the kiln with good, active ventilation
- 1 firing surface, kiln pad, or firebrick
- 1 small fireproof container (terracotta flower pot saucer or stainless-steel shallow bowl, for example)
- alumina hydrate (enough to fill the small fireproof container)
- 1 small cup or scoop
- 1 good-quality dust mask or respirator (for fine particulates)
- 1 pair vinyl or latex gloves
- 1 pair long barbecue tongs
- 1 barbecue spatula
- 1 pair extra-heavy leather work gloves or potter's gloves (fire retardant)
- 1 large stainless-steel bowl filled with cool water
- 1 pair long steel tweezers

MAKING THE MOLD

1. Use different hands to remove equal-size lumps from each of the jars of the two-part silicone mold-making material. (If you use the same hand, you could accidentally transfer material from one jar to the other, which would prematurely begin the curing, or hardening.) Each lump should be nearly twice as large as the model.

2. Although you have 10 to 30 minutes before the materials begins to cure, quickly combine the two lumps, kneading and twisting the material until the combined material is one color.

3. Roll the material into a sphere and place it on the single playing card, flattening it very slightly.

4. Press the model into the mold-making material, making certain not to press it so deeply that it breaks through to the work surface. If it does, and the mold material is still soft, remove the model and try again. If the material has already begun to cure and is not pliable, discard it and begin again with fresh material. Otherwise, keep the model in place.

5. Set the mold aside, with the model still in place, and allow the material to cure for 15 to 45 minutes. Depending on the type of material, the curing time can vary. The material is cured when it's firm—test that your fingernail doesn't leave a permanent impression.

6. When the mold material has cured, gently pop out the model **(A)**. (Belicold has its own lubrication, which makes it easy to remove the model. If you are working with another material, see page 147.)

MAKING THE GRANULES

1. While the mold is curing, tape the dull edge of the tissue blade for visibility, and carefully and lightly lubricate the sharp edge and then your hands with the olive oil and the sponge. Lightly oil the 1/8" (3 mm) -diameter clay cutter or brass tubing, the roller, and the work surface.

2. Remove a lump of PMC Standard, about 1/4" (6 mm) in diameter, from the package. Return the excess metal clay to the package or plastic wrap.

3. Place one three-card stack of playing cards near each of the edges of the work surface. Place the lump of PMC Standard between the two stacks. With the roller, roll the lump into a sheet, level with the height of the cards.

4. Punch out four circles using the 1/8" (3 mm) -diameter clay cutter or tubing. If the circles get stuck inside the cutter, push them out with a scribe or toothpick. If you want more granules, repeat the process to increase the number of circles. Working carefully with the tissue blade, lift off the excess metal clay and return it to the package or just wrap it in plastic wrap.

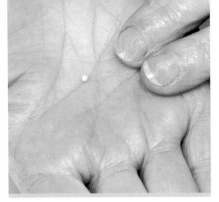

B. Roll cut circles of clay into small sphere to make as many granules as you'd like for your bead.

5. Working quickly, lift each circle off the work surface and roll it between the palms of your hands to form a small round sphere (**B**).

6. Set the spheres onto the mug warmer to dry or allow them to air-dry.

MAKING THE SIDES OF THE BEAD

1. Lightly oil the cured mold, your hands, the paper clip, and the work surface.

2. Gather a lump of PMC Standard slightly larger than the size of the depression in your mold. Return the excess metal clay to the package or plastic wrap.

3. If the mold is deep (like the one I used), press or roll a small point on it (**C**). Place the point into the mold and press the metal clay deeply into the mold with your index finger. Allow the excess metal clay to ooze out around your finger.

4. Remove your finger and trim off some of the excess metal clay. Place the excess metal clay in the package or plastic wrap. Leave a rim or flange on the outside of the molded metal clay.

5. If you want to save a little metal clay, use the bent leg of the paper clip to shave away some in the depressed molded area (**D**). The depression will be inside the bead and not visible after the bead is assembled. Be careful not to thin the bead too much. Save the excess metal clay in the package or plastic wrap.

Tip

Instead of working with a paper clip, you can shave the excess metal clay in the mold depression with an art knife—but be sure to work very carefully, moving the sharp blade away from your fingers.

C. Press the metal clay into the mold, allowing the excess to ooze out around your finger.

D. Rather than waste metal clay, trim the excess around the mold depression with the leg of the paper clip.

E. Dry the two sides of the bead on a mug warmer, turning them over occasionally to allow the insides to dry, too. They are relatively thick and may take a while to dry completely.

F. The hole supports are very thin and fragile, so lift them carefully off the work surface. Drape them on a cutter or a piece of brass tubing that rests on the mug warmer.

G. Carefully file the center depression in the bead, frequently checking depth and width with the skewer.

6. Carefully remove the first side of your bead from the mold. The silicone will be somewhat pliable, which makes it easier to release the clay from the mold.

7. Set the bead side aside to dry on the mug warmer (**E**). At this stage, the edges will look messy, even though it's trimmed, but you'll refine the shape later.

8. Repeat steps 2–7 to make the other side of the bead.

9. After the bead sides are dry, sand and refine their edges.

MAKING THE HOLE SUPPORTS

1. After taping the dull edge of the tissue blade for visibility, carefully and lightly lubricate the sharp edge and then your hands with the olive oil and the sponge. Lightly oil the work surface, the roller, and the clay cutters or brass tubing.

2. Place a ¼" (6 mm)-diameter lump of metal clay on the work surface and place three-card stack of cards on either side of it. With the roller, roll the lump into a sheet, level with the height of the cards.

3. Cut two holes with the smaller-diameter cutter or tubing, about ½" (12 mm) apart. If the tubing did not remove the metal clay from the hole, lift it out with the tip of the skewer or a scribe and return it to the package or plastic wrap.

4. Cut two circles with the larger-diameter cutter or tubing, centering each one over the holes made in step 3.

5. Carefully pull off the excess metal clay with the tissue blade. Carefully lift the fragile hole supports off the work surface by gently sliding the tissue blade around the edges of the supports until they lift easily from the work surface.

6. Lay the large-diameter clay cutter or brass tubing on the mug warmer. Dry the hole supports by draping them on the side of the cutter or tubing, adjusting them to fit the curve (**F**). Allow them to dry completely.

JOINING THE BEAD SIDES

1. When the bead sides are completely dry, sand the edges of each so they sit flat on the work surface.

2. Place the two bead sides together to check for size and alignment. Adjust the fit by sanding—you'll have another chance to adjust later, too.

3. Now, create the depth and width of the bead hole. With the flat edge of one of the skewer sides facing up, rest the skewer across the surface of the bead. Make a pencil mark on the bead to indicate the outer edges of the bead.

4. Remove the skewer. With the round file, carefully file out a center depression in the bead that is no deeper than one-half the diameter of the skewer and no wider than the pencil-marked area (**G**). Check frequently, using the skewer as a guide, to avoid filing too large a hole.

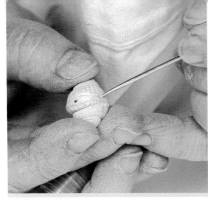

H. Create four slight depressions in the metal clay bead by twirling the scribe point into the moistened area.

I. Apply slip to each of the four depressions you've made in the bead and press each granule into place.

J. Join the supports to the bead one at a time, "gluing" them in place with slip.

5. Repeat steps 1–4 to create a depression in the other bead side.

6. Moisten the edges of both bead sides with the filled waterbrush or wet paintbrush.

7. Add slip to the edge of one of the bead sides and press both sides together. Rotate the joint slightly to secure it and then realign.

8. Set the joined bead sides aside to dry on the mug warmer.

9. Sand and refine the joint with salon boards or emery paper, beginning with coarse grits and ending with fine.

ADDING THE GRANULES

1. With the pencil, mark four evenly spaced locations around the circumference of the joined bead sides, along the joint. Avoid the area near the hole.

2. Moisten one of the marks with the filled waterbrush or wet paintbrush and wait a few moments. Then twirl the point of a scribe in the moistened spot to create a very slight depression and reactivate the metal clay (**H**). Continue to apply water and rotate the shaper until you "bring up" some slip from the reactivated clay.

3. Apply slip in the depression with the small shaper.

4. Holding one of the granules with the tweezers, moisten a spot on the granule with the waterbrush or wet paintbrush.

5. Press the granule into the slip in the depression. Rotate the granule very slightly with your finger and firmly press it onto the depression.

6. Repeat steps 2–5, joining the remaining three granules to the bead sides on the marks (**I**).

ADDING THE HOLE SUPPORT

1. Check all the edges of the bead and hole supports and sand and refine where needed.

2. On one side of the bead, moisten the area right around the hole.

3. Moisten the concave side of one of the hole supports.

4. With the shaper, add a small amount of slip to the moistened area on the bead.

5. Lift one of the hole supports with the tweezers. Place it, moistened side down, on the slip around the hole. Rotate and then realign the cap to make a firm joint (**J**).

6. Repeat steps 2–5 to position the second hole support. Set the bead aside to dry.

7. When the bead is completely dry, check for flaws and refine them as needed. Pop off any excess slip with the art knife. You can reconstitute the dried slip with water to make homemade slip. Sand again.

FIRING THE MOLD-FORMED BEAD

1. Place the firing surface, kiln pad, or fire-brick in a cold kiln. Place a water-filled fireproof container near the kiln.

2. Place the bead on the surface and close the kiln door.

3. Turn on the kiln and select the program that will allow the kiln to run for two hours at 1650°F (900°C).

4. After the kiln has completed the firing cycle, allow it to cool down a little. Open the door to allow it to cool down even more.

5. Check the digital readout of the temperature on the kiln and, after the kiln has cooled down, put on the heavy gloves and move the bead with tweezers either to another fireproof surface to air-cool or into a large stainless-steel bowl filled with cool water to quench it.

6. Finish and polish bead (see page 25).

photo: Sabine Alienor Singery

Bulan Bola

ARTIST: Sabine Alienor Singery
MATERIAL: fine silver
TECHNIQUES: metal clay, hollow-core construction (cork clay), granulation
DIMENSIONS: ¾" diameter (2 cm)

Draped
BEAD
with 22k Gold

SKILL LEVEL: Intermediate to advanced
FINISHED SIZE: 1¼" high × 1" wide × ⅜" deep
(32 mm × 25 mm × 10 mm)

"Metal clay can hold a draped, three-dimensional form."

This Bead

makes the most of one of the best features of metal clay—its ability to assume and retain a shape or form while draped on a three-dimensional support or armature. The basic concept was introduced by J. Fred Woell, one of the original and ongoing senior instructors in PMC, who taught one of the first PMC workshops in the United States.

This project also explores three additional techniques: working with PMC+, carving a silicone printing block to make a printing plate for metal clay, and applying 22k gold PMC appliqué elements. The 22k gold PMC creates a beautiful contrast with the fine silver of PMC+. (If you prefer not to use 22k gold PMC, you can substitute PMC+.)

What You Will Need

- about 25 g of PMC+
- 1 (3 g) package of 22k gold PMC
- 1 container of PMC+ slip
- 1 clean piece of flat wood, about 6" × 4" (15 × 10 cm) (Some hobby stores sell finished wooden plaques.)
- 1 wooden dowel, at least 18" (45 cm) long and ¼" to ⅜" (6–9 mm) in diameter
- wood glue
- assorted wood clamps
- 1 very soft black lead pencil
- 1 Safety-Kut or other rubber printing block, no smaller than 3" (7.5 cm) square
- linoleum carvers or cutters
- 1 small V-shaped blade for the linoleum carver
- 1 small bottle of olive oil (or other suitable lubricant)
- 1 piece of cellulose kitchen sponge, 1" (25 mm) square
- 1 porcelain or stainless-steel saucer or similar container (for the oiled sponge)
- 1 piece 220-grit emery or sandpaper, about 3" (7.5 cm) square
- 2 four-card stacks of playing cards
- assorted loose playing cards
- 1 circle cutter, 1½" (3.8 cm) in diameter
- 1 hair dryer
- 1 mug warmer
- 1 jeweler's or leather-design stamping punch or letterpress ornament
- assorted salon boards or wet/dry emery papers in fine and coarse grits
- 1 color or clay shaper
- 2 three-card stacks of playing cards

The finished Draped Bead strung as a pendant on necklace of amazonite beads.

"At the end of each successfully completed step, I mentally acknowledge it by simply saying to myself or out loud: 'Thank you!' Just saying 'Thank you!' does something significant to my personal energy. It keeps me rolling." J. Fred Woell

A. This armature is made with dowels of two different diameters glued to one board.

B. Carve the design in the block, making sure to move the blade of the linoleum carver away from the hand that's holding the block.

C. The soft block is easily carved.

- 1 brass clay cutter or short length of brass tubing, about ³/₁₆" (5 mm) in diameter
- 1 brass clay cutter or short length of brass tubing, about ⁵/₈" (15 mm) in diameter
- assorted short lengths of brass tubing or circle cutter to fit over silver/gold unit (see instructions)
- 1 art knife (X-Acto, for example)
- 1 PMC kiln
- 1 fireproof surface for the kiln with good, active ventilation
- 1 Kaowool insulated firing pad, 6" (15 cm) square
- 1 firing surface, kiln pad, or firebrick
- 1 pair long barbecue tongs
- 1 barbecue spatula
- 1 pair extra-heavy leather work gloves or potter's gloves (fire retardant)
- 1 large stainless-steel bowl filled with cool water
- 1 pair long steel tweezers

MAKING THE ARMATURE

1. Cut the dowel into three 6" (15 cm) lengths. You can cut the dowel to length with a jeweler's saw, keyhole saw, or any other type of saw that works. You can even clip the dowel pieces with a pair of side cutters—but if you do, cut the pieces a little longer to allow for the wasted ends where the wood has been clipped and crushed. Then sand the ends flat.

2. Glue the dowels to the flat piece of wood, spaced about ³/₈" (10 mm) apart. Clamp them in place until the glue is completely dry.

   NOTE: The different sizes of dowels used for this armature allow me to vary the depth of the metal-clay-draped forms **(A)**. You can also vary the distance between the dowels or even glue at angles instead of parallel to each other.

MAKING THE PRINTING PLATE

1. With the black lead pencil, draw a series of closely spaced, wavy lines on the Safety-Kut or rubber printing block.

2. Insert the V-shaped blade in the linoleum carver. Handle the sharp blade very carefully.

3. Holding the printing block with one hand and the linoleum carver with the other, carve all the lines in the printing block. Be sure to carve away from the hand that's holding the block **(B)**. You won't have to push very hard—the block is quite soft **(C)**.

4. Thoroughly clean up the carving residue. You don't want to confuse the small bits of block material with bits of dried metal clay that may accumulate later in the process.

MAKING THE DRAPED FORMS

1. When the dowel armature is dry, oil it, the roller, the emery paper, the circle cutter, and your hands. Oil the printing plate, too, being sure to press oil into the carved depressions.

2. Place the printing plate on the surface of your bench. Place one four-card stack of playing cards on each side of it. Add playing cards or other flat boards underneath each stack to raise it completely above the surface of the printing block. (I used small sheets of Plexiglas and extra playing cards.)

3. Remove a lump of PMC+ from the package and roll it into a ball about 1" (2.5 cm) in diameter.

4. With the palm of your hand, flatten the ball on the printing block. With the roller, very firmly roll the metal clay into a sheet, level with height of the four-card stack. If the metal clay sheet doesn't seem wide enough, roll once, then turn the printing plate 90 degrees and roll it again to the four-card level. Leave the metal clay on the printing block and the four-card stacks in place.

5. Place the emery paper, grit side down, on the surface of the metal clay sheet. Roll the emery paper into the metal clay.

6. Remove the emery paper, but don't move the metal clay.

7. Cut out one circle from the metal clay sheet with the 1½" (3.8 cm)-diameter circle cutter.

8. Lift the metal clay circle off the printing block and drape it on the armature, with the printed side face up.

Tip

In place of the circle cutter, you can use a small juice or shot glass to make the draped forms. Trim the clay sheet around the rim of the glass with a sewing needle.

Gently adjust the circle to conform to the curve of the dowels and the spaces between them, pushing the circle at its edges to avoid distorting the printed pattern **(D)**.

9. Repeat steps 2–8 to make the second draped form.

10. Set the armature aside to allow the draped forms to dry. At this stage, dry them with a hair dryer. When the forms are firm and nearly dry, you can carefully lift them off the armature and place them on the mug warmer to finish drying.

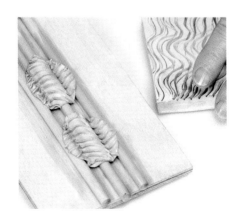

D. The forms take shape as they dry on the dowel armature.

MAKING THE END CAPS

1. Oil the work surface, your hands and the roller. Remove a small ball of PMC+ from the package and roll out a three-card thick sheet of PMC+.

2. Cut out two circles with the ³/₁₆" (5 mm)-diameter brass tubing or clay cutter.

3. Cut a larger circle with the ⁵/₈" (15 mm)-diameter brass tubing or clay cutter, centering it over the holes made in step 2, to make a flattened doughnut.

4. Place the circles on the mug warmer to dry completely. Check them occasionally for warping and flatten them if needed.

5. When the circles are completely dry, sand and refine the edges.

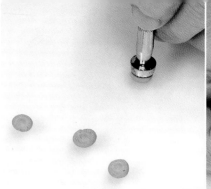

E. Flatten the gold metal clay ball slightly as you press the stamping punch or letterpress ornament.

F. Hold the forms together to check the join of the curved surfaces. Sand as needed.

MAKING THE APPLIQUÉ UNITS

1. Oil the work surface and the jeweler's or leather-design stamping punch or letterpress ornament.

2. Before unwrapping the 22k gold PMC, read the instructions on the package. Knead the metal clay while it is still wrapped. If it still seems stiff when you unwrap it, add a very small amount of water—one small drop—to the clay, as directed. Allow the clay to absorb the water. If you need to add more, add only one drop at a time.

3. Roll the gold metal clay into a ball. Working carefully with the tissue blade, divide the ball into four equal sections.

4. Roll each section into a ball and press the punch or ornament into each ball, flattening it slightly (**E**). Place the flattened balls on the mug warmer to dry.

6. When the four gold elements are completely dry, you can begin to form the framework that will surround them. Remove a small amount of PMC+ from the package, roll it into a ball, and place it on the work surface.

7. Press one of the gold balls into the fresh silver PMC+ ball until the gold ball is just below the surface of the silver ball. The silver becomes a frame for the gold.

8. With a skewer or similar tool, press four equally spaced depressions around the circumference of the silver ball, moving the silver clay toward the gold ball.

9. Use a short length of round brass tubing or a round cutter to press down on and trim the silver-framed gold to form a circle (the tubing or cutter circumference should match the outer edges of the silver frame).

10. Set the silver/gold unit on the mug warmer to dry. Repeat steps 6–10 with the remaining gold balls.

JOINING THE FORMS, APPLIQUÉ ELEMENTS, AND END CAPS

1. When the draped forms are completely dry, sand and refine the edges with salon boards or emery papers.

2. Hold the two forms together, printed sides face out. Check the join of the curves and sand each form lightly as needed with 220-grit emery paper (**F**).

3. With the filled waterbrush or wet paintbrush, lightly moisten the flat, sanded areas.

4. With the shaper, apply PMC+ slip to the moistened area on one form. Gently press the two forms together. If the forms don't meet perfectly at the join, reinforce them with additional fresh clay on the inside of the joint.

Tip

To sand the forms easily, lay the emery paper on a flat surface. Place one draped form on the paper, with the printed side up. Move the form back and forth, without pressing hard, to create an area that's slightly flat. Don't sand so much that you sand through the form. If you do sand too much, just add slip to those spots—on the unprinted side—allowing the slip to squish through to the textured side. Smooth the slip with a shaper and allow to dry.

G. Sand the bottom edges of each appliqué unit to shape them to match the curve of the draped form.

H. Secure the end caps to each end of the form with water and slip.

FIRING THE BEAD

1. Place the Kaowool firing pad on the firing surface, kiln pad, or firebrick in a cold kiln.

2. Place the bead on the firing pad and close the kiln door.

3. Both fine silver PMC+ and 22k gold PMC have compatible firing temperatures of 1650°F (900°C) for 10 minutes or 1560°F (850°C) for 30 minutes. We're going to fire at the higher temperature but leave the kiln running for 30 minutes to assure a good, strong bead. Turn the kiln on and select the program that will allow the kiln to run for 30 minutes at 1650°F (900°C).

4. After the kiln has completed the firing cycle, allow it to cool down a little. Then open the door to allow it to cool down even more.

5. Check the digital readout of the temperature on the kiln and, after the kiln has cooled down, put on the heavy gloves and move the bead with tweezers either to another fireproof surface to air-cool or into a large stainless-steel bowl filled with cool water to quench it.

6. Finish and polish bead (see page 25).

5. When the gold appliqué units are completely dry, refine and sand the edges. First, however, decide where you'd like to place the units on the assembled form. The bottom edges of the units must be shaped to closely match the curved surface of those areas of the form **(G)**.

6. Lightly moisten the bottom of one of the appliqué units. Then moisten the area on the form where you'll place the unit.

7. Add a substantial dollop of PMC+ slip to the moistened spot. Press the appliqué unit to that spot, rotating it gently to secure the joint.

8. Repeat steps 6–7 with the remaining three appliqué units.

9. Place the bead on the mug warmer to dry completely.

10. Refine the hole ends of the dry bead with a salon board, making them flat and parallel to each other.

11. To strengthen the joint between the form halves, add fresh PMC+ to the inside of the joint. Roll a thin snakelike coil of PMC+ and insert it into the hole of the bead. With a small shaper, press the fresh metal clay into the joint and smooth it against the joint.

12. Lightly moisten one end of the form and one side of one of the end caps. Add slip to the bead and press the end cap onto it, rotating it slightly to secure the joint **(H)**. Place it on the mug warmer to dry. Repeat this step to secure the other end cap.

13. When the bead is completely dry, remove excess slip with the art knife and smooth with salon boards. Add more slip where needed and dry completely. Sand and refine any flaws in the surface.

Draped Taper Bead

ARTIST: Linda Kaye-Moses

MATERIALS: fine silver, sterling silver, antique African glass beads

TECHNIQUES: metal clay, photopolymer- and carved-plate printing, draping (armature), patination

DIMENSIONS: 2⅜" long × ⅞" at largest diameter (6 cm × 2.3 cm)

Lentil Bead

ARTIST: Sabine Alienor Singery

MATERIALS: fine silver

TECHNIQUES: hollow-core construction, draping (light bulb), patination

DIMENSIONS: 1⅜" (3.5 cm) diameter

Ribbon
BEAD

SKILL LEVEL: Intermediate to advanced
FINISHED SIZE: 5/8" diameter × 7/8" wide
(16 mm × 22 mm)

"The Ribbon Bead is a hollow, openwork bead."

There are many ways to construct hollow metal clay beads. Some are constructed without an inner support, or core; others, like this Ribbon Bead, are constructed with a support. There are several types of cores. Some of the simplest are made from readily available materials, such as paper or bread dough (see page 18).

In this project, you'll learn how to make a strip, or ribbon, hollow bead. The core is built with moistened bread, coated in a layer of wax, which will support metal clay strips (ribbons). The strips, which have a triangular cross section, are made with a small clay extruder. You can make a ribbon bead without an extruder, but the extruder easily creates the cross sections, a detail that adds interest to the bead—and which would be more complicated to make without the extruder.

The finished Ribbon Bead centered on a strand of oval amethyst beads , strung on hand-knotted silk.

"You will do foolish things. But do them with enthusiasm." Colette

What You Will Need

- 8–10 g of PMC3
- 1 container of PMC3 slip
- casting wax pellets
- 1 small double boiler (or small saucepan with a lid and a bowl that sits inside the pan)
- 1 hot plate
- 1 pot holder
- 1 slice of soft white bread
- 1 toothpick
- wax files, coarse and fine
- 1 coarse salon board
- 1 work surface (tempered glass or Plexiglas)
- 1 steel drill bit, size #21 (with pin vise to hold drill bit, optional)
- 1 steel drill bit, size #46–50, depending on the bead hole diameter needed
- running water
- assorted toothpicks, paper lollipop sticks, or scribe
- 1 art knife (X-Acto, for example)
- 1 small bottle of olive oil (or other suitable lubricant)
- 1 piece of cellulose kitchen sponge, 1" (25 mm) square
- 1 porcelain or stainless-steel saucer or similar container (for the oiled sponge)
- 1 waterbrush (or small container of water and fine-tipped sable paintbrush)
- 1 Makin's Ultimate Clay Extruder or other small clay extruder and a die with triangular opening
- 1 jeweler's or leather-design stamping punch or letterpress ornament
- 1 tissue blade
- 1 color or clay shaper
- 1 plastic roller
- 2 three-card stacks of playing cards
- 1 mug warmer
- assorted salon boards or wet/dry emery paper in several grits

A. This project was made with a spherical core, an easy shape to work with, but you can follow the same process to create a core of almost any shape, as long as you can mold the bread dough to conform.

B. Coat the bread-dough form with a thin layer of wax.

- 1 small fireproof container (a terra-cotta flowerpot saucer or shallow stainless-steel bowl, for example)
- alumina hydrate (enough to fill the small fireproof container)
- 1 small cup or scoop
- 1 good-quality dust mask or respirator (for fine particulates)
- 1 pair vinyl or latex gloves
- 1 PMC kiln
- 1 fireproof surface for the kiln with good, active ventilation
- 1 firing surface, kiln pad, or firebrick
- 1 pair long barbecue tongs
- 1 barbecue spatula
- 1 pair extra-heavy leather work gloves or potter's gloves (fire retardant)
- 1 large stainless-steel bowl filled with cool water
- 1 pair long steel tweezers
- 1 black lead pencil

MAKING THE CORE

1. Add water to the bottom pot of the double boiler. Add wax pellets to the top pot, to a depth of at least 3" (7.5 cm). Place the double boiler on the hotplate and turn the heat setting to "high." When the water comes to a full boil, reduce the heat so that the water continues to simmer. (If there is too much water in the lower pot and it boils over, use the potholder to remove the top pot, pour out some of the water in the bottom pot, and then replace the top pot. Repeat as needed.) Let the wax melt completely—about 15 to 20 minutes.

2. Lightly moisten a small bit of bread and form it into a sphere (or another shape if you prefer). The bread should not be soggy—you should not be able to squeeze out drops of water. If it is, start again with a new piece.

3. Push a toothpick partway into the sphere to form a small handle **(A)**.

4. After the wax has melted, hold the bread by the toothpick handle and dip the bread sphere into the wax, coating it completely. Remove the sphere from

> **Tip**
>
> When melting wax, check the pan often to prevent the water from boiling over or boiling away completely. If the water evaporates, the wax could flare and cause a fire. If you need to add water, always handle the pot with a pot holder.

the wax quickly, so that the thin coating of wax begins to cool and harden **(B)**. Refine the shape a little with your fingers, removing any drips of wax. Don't worry about the bead holes for now.

5. Remove the toothpick from the sphere. Let the sphere cool completely and then refine it with first the coarse and then the medium wax files.

6. Now you'll remove the bread dough from the wax core. Rest the sphere on a clean work surface. Stabilize the sphere with one hand and rest the drill bit against the wax surface.

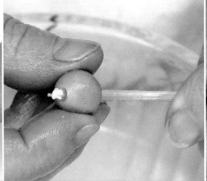
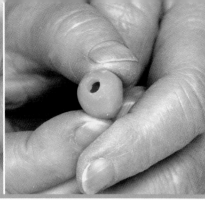

C. Carefully drill two holes on opposite ends to remove the bread dough from the wax core.

D. The bread core must be entirely washed out to prevent it from flaring in the kiln, which might raise the temperature in and around the metal clay.

E. When the bread core is removed, you'll have a hollow wax sphere that you'll cover with ribbons of metal clay to form the bead.

7. Without pressing too hard, rotate the drill bit, cutting into the surface. If it's rotating in the correct direction, you'll be removing curved bits of wax (**C**). Carefully drill through the wax, allowing the drill bit to do its job, without exerting too much pressure, until the drill bit breaks through to the interior.

8. Repeat steps 6 and 7 to drill a hole opposite the one you just drilled. Clean all wax debris off your work surface.

9. Now, you'll remove the bread from the core. Immerse the sphere under warm water (not hot, or it will melt the wax again) and let the water soak into the bread core. Agitate the sphere to make sure that the water gets into it.

10. When you remove the sphere from the water, the bread should dissolve and release from the wax. Shake the sphere under running water to completely remove the bread core. If there's any bread left inside the wax sphere, you can blow it out one of the holes and use the toothpicks, paper lollipop sticks, or a scribe to push and scrape out the remaining pieces (**D, E**).

MAKING THE CIRCULAR RIBBON

1. After taping the dull edge of the tissue blade for visibility, carefully and lightly lubricate the sharp edge and then your hands with the olive oil and sponge. Lightly oil the extruder, the die, the work surface, and the stamping punch or letterpress ornament.

2. Place a lump of PMC3, ⅝" (16 mm) in diameter, in the extruder. Insert the die into the extruder cap and screw on the cap.

3. Holding the cap end of the extruder over the work surface, rotate the extruder handle (or push it, depending on the style). The PMC will exit in a continuous, triangular strip (**F**). (If the edges of the extruded clay develop small cracks, the clay is drying too quickly. Remove all the metal clay from the extruder and add a little glycerin to it [see page 15]. Then begin step 3 again.) Extrude a length of PMC that is long enough to wrap around the wax sphere, allowing a little overlap at the ends (less than ⅛"[3 mm]). With the tissue blade, slice off the metal clay flush with the extruder opening.

Tip

If you don't have an extruder, you can roll out a sheet of metal clay (4 cards thick) and cut flat ribbon strips with the tissue blade. These strips can be sanded to create a triangular cross section.

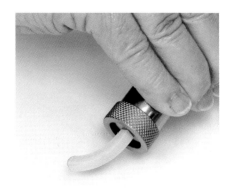

F. The triangular shape in the die opening gives the metal clay ribbon its shape. Extrude a ribbon long enough to wrap around the sphere, with overlapping ends.

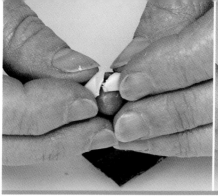
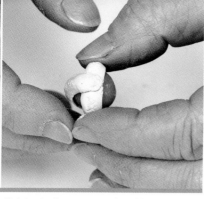

G. Bevel the overlapping ends of the ribbon and join them with a little PMC slip.

H. Join the first semicircular ribbon to the circular ribbon on the wax sphere.

Tip

Here are two alternate ways of applying design to the ribbon of metal clay. Make shallow depressions along the length of the ribbon with the tip of the shaper. Or make shallow lines across the width of the ribbon with the edge of a salon board or ruler.

4. Stand the extruder upright on a damp piece of paper towel and a layer of plastic wrap to prevent the metal clay that's still in the extruder from drying out.

5. Wrap the ribbon strip around the sphere, overlapping the ends. Don't worry about covering the holes in the sphere. You'll make the true bead holes later. Working carefully with the tissue blade, trim the overlapping ends at an oblique angle or bevel (**G**).

6. Apply a little PMC slip on one of the beveled ends with the shaper. Bring the two ends together and press lightly with the shaper to join. Try to maintain the shape of the strip.

7. Working with the punch or ornament, gently press a design along the length of the triangular strip. As you create the design, you will also be slightly stretching the strip so that, as it dries and shrinks, the joint won't tear open.

8. Set the bead aside to air-dry. (Do not dry with a hair dryer or mug warmer or you'll melt the wax.)

MAKING SEMICIRCULAR RIBBONS

1. When the circular ribbon is completely dry, extrude more triangular PMC ribbon or roll and cut strips to form a semicircular ribbon. The ribbon should be a little longer than the length needed to reach from one 'pole' of the sphere to the other, meeting the circular ribbon at both points.

2. With the punch or ornament, gently press a design along the length of the triangular strip.

3. Lightly flatten (thin) each end of the ribbon with the roller. Trim the width at the ribbon ends to match the width of the rest of the length.

4. With the shaper, add a little slip to the joined ends of the circular ribbon. Add another small amount to a spot on the ribbon just opposite that joint. Drape the semicircular ribbon around the sphere, placing one flattened end on each of the slipped spots. Press each end firmly, but don't stretch the ribbon too much (**H**).

5. Partially air-dry this ribbon. Then repeat steps 1–4 to make a second semicircular ribbon for the opposite side of the wax sphere. Join the ends of this ribbon to the ends of the first one (**I**). Again, allow the ribbon to air-dry completely.

I. The two overlapping semicircular ribbons are joined to the circular ribbon with slip.

MAKING THE LARGE AND SMALL HOLE SUPPORTS

1. After taping the dull edge of the tissue blade for visibility, carefully and lightly lubricate the sharp edge and then your hands with the olive oil and the sponge. Lightly oil the work surface and roller.

2. Roll a small lump of PMC to form a ball about ½" (13 mm) in diameter. Place it on your work surface and flatten it slightly with your finger.

3. Place a three-card stack of playing cards on either side of the flattened lump. With the roller, roll the lump into a sheet, level with the height of the cards.

4. Work carefully with the tissue blade to cut out two small squares, about ³/₈" (9 mm) square.

5. Use your fingers to form each of the squares into a slightly domed shape. Place them on the mug warmer to dry.

6. Repeat steps 2–5, this time making the squares ¼" (6 mm) square.

JOINING THE HOLE SUPPORTS TO THE RIBBONS

1. When ribbons are completely dry, work with salon boards or emery paper to sand and smooth the joints where the circular and semicircular ribbons meet.

2. Moisten the inner curve (concave side) of the larger hole supports with the filled waterbrush or wet paintbrush. Wait about 30 seconds and repeat. The water will make the hole supports slightly pliable so that you can fit them to the ribbon joints. While you're waiting, also moisten the outside of the ribbon joints.

3. With the shaper, apply slip to the inner curve of one of the larger hole supports. Press this support onto one of the ribbon joints. Repeat for the remaining larger hole supports.

4. Repeat steps 2 and 3 with the smaller hole supports.

5. Allow the joints to air-dry completely. Then pop off the excess dried slip with an art knife or a scribe. Refine the ribbon bead with salon boards or emery paper.

J. The bead hole is drilled through the hole support, ribbons, and wax core.

DRILLING THE HOLES

1. Choose a size #46–50 drill bit, depending on the diameter of the hole you'll need to string the bead on your chain, cord, cable, or ribbon.

2. Make a pencil mark at the center of each hole support.

3. Gently rest the bead on a clean work surface with one hole support facing up.

4. Stabilize the bead with one hand and rest the drill bit on the pencil mark. Without pressing too hard, rotate the drill bit, cutting into the surface of the hole support. When the drill bit is rotating in the correct direction, you'll be removing small curved bits of dried metal clay from the support. (You can add these bits and any sanding dust to your homemade slip.)

5. Carefully drill through the hole support and the ribbon joint, allowing the drill bit to do its job, without exerting too much pressure. In this greenware (unfired) state, the bead is somewhat fragile, and too much pressure could crack it.

6. When the drill bit has broken through to the interior of the bead, continue rotating the drill while carefully backing it out of the hole. After you've removed the bit, you'll be able to see the wax core through the hole.

7. Turn over the bead and repeat steps 3–6 for the second hole support (**J**).

8. If the holes have any ragged edges, smooth them by twirling a little water in the holes with the color shaper. Set the bead aside to dry again.

9. Sand and refine any irregularities in the bead. Check for gaps and fill with slip or fresh PMC3. Dry completely and refine again.

FIRING THE RIBBON BEAD

1. Put on a respirator or a good dust mask and vinyl gloves. Fill the small container with alumina hydrate.

2. Place the bead on the alumina hydrate. Then place the container on a firing surface, kiln pad, or firebrick in a cold kiln. Close the kiln door.

3. Turn on the kiln and select the program that will allow the kiln to run for 2 hours at 1650°F (900°C). PMC3 can be fired at lower temperatures for a shorter period of time, but the longer and hotter schedule will produce a stronger bead.

4. After the kiln has completed the firing cycle, allow it to cool down a little. Then open the door to allow it to cool down even more.

5. Check the digital readout of the temperature on the kiln and, after the kiln has cooled down, put on the heavy gloves and move the bead with tweezers either to another fireproof surface to air-cool or into a large stainless-steel bowl filled with cool water to quench it.

6. Finish and polish bead (see page 25).

Small Ribbon Bead

ARTIST: Linda Kaye-Moses
MATERIALS: fine silver, sterling silver, beryl beads
TECHNIQUES: dry construction, hollow core ribbon construction
DIMENSIONS: ¾" long × ½" diameter (20 mm × 13 mm)

Tubular
BEAD #2

SKILL LEVEL: Intermediate to advanced
FINISHED SIZE: ⅜" high × 1" wide × ¼" deep
(10 mm × 25 mm × 6 mm)

> "PMC Standard
> makes a light weight
> tubular bead."

Tubular
Bead #2 is made with PMC Standard

(sometimes called Original). Although the walls of the bead are somewhat thick, PMC Standard ensures a lightweight bead. In this project, you'll make two parts of the bead with the Makin's Ultimate Clay Extruder: the tube element and the spiral coil. This type of extruder not only can produce long coils with a range of cross sections, but can also create tube forms, allowing you to make instant beads. The Makin's extruder is a useful tool to add to your toolbox, for this project and for many future projects, too. If you don't own this extruder, however, there's an alternative method for making this bead described in the sidebar on page 76.

What You Will Need

- 5–6 g of PMC Standard (also known as Original)
- 1 small package of polymer clay, any color
- 1 syringe of PMC3
- 1 small bottle of olive oil (or other suitable lubricant)
- 1 piece of cellulose kitchen sponge, 1" (25 mm) square
- 1 porcelain or stainless-steel saucer or similar container (for the oiled sponge)
- 1 work surface (tempered glass or Plexiglas)
- 1 Makin's Ultimate Clay Extruder, a hollow-core extrusion adapter (largest hole), diamond-shaped die, and a small-diameter circular die (If you do not have an extruder or a hollow-core adapter, follow the instructions in the sidebar on page 76 for hand-building the bead.)

- 1 tissue blade
- 1 mug warmer
- 1 plastic roller
- 2 five-card stacks of playing cards
- 1 brass clay cutter or short length of brass tubing, about ⅛" (3 mm) in diameter
- 1 brass clay cutter or short length of brass tubing, about ⅜" (9 mm) in diameter
- 1 ruler
- 1 pair scissors
- 1 black lead pencil
- 1 playing card
- 2 marbles or stone beads, each about ¾" (19 mm) in diameter
- 2 three-card stacks of playing cards

The finished Tubular Bead #2 with cylindrical turquoise beads, strung on hand-knotted silk.

"Making art is 'the fire down there that makes the thing.'"
Andy Goldsworthy

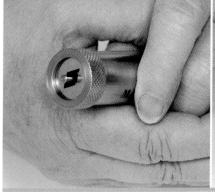

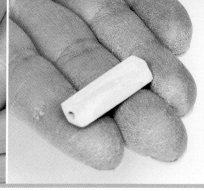

A. The pin on the hollow-core adapter should be centered on the diamond-shaped die opening.

B. Extrude 1" (25 mm) of metal clay and slice it flush with the opening in the extruder end.

- 1 waterbrush (or small container of water and fine-tipped sable paintbrush)
- small pieces of paper towels
- 1 art knife (X-Acto, for example)
- assorted salon boards or wet/dry emery paper in several grits
- 1 PMC kiln
- 1 fireproof surface for the kiln with good, active ventilation
- 1 Kaowool insulated firing pad, 6" (15 cm) square
- 1 firing surface, kiln pad, or firebrick
- 1 pair long barbecue tongs
- 1 barbecue spatula
- 1 pair extra-heavy leather work gloves or potter's gloves (fire retardant)
- 1 large stainless-steel bowl filled with cool water
- 1 pair long steel tweezers

MAKING THE TUBE ELEMENT

1. After taping the dull edge of the tissue blade for visibility, carefully and lightly lubricate the sharp edge and then your hands with the olive oil and the sponge. Lightly oil your work surface, the Makin's Ultimate Clay Extruder, the hollow-core adapter, and the dies. (If you do not have a Makin's extruder, follow the instructions in the sidebar on the following page.)

2. Remove a lump of PMC Standard about the size of a large marble, about 1⅛" (29 mm) in diameter. Wrap the rest of the metal clay and return it to the original package.

3. Place the die in the bottom cap of the extruder.

4. Load the metal clay into the extruder from the bottom of the barrel.

5. Insert the hollow-core adapter into the barrel of the extruder, up against the metal clay, with the pin facing away from the metal clay.

6. Partially screw on the cap and adjust the die so that the pin on the adapter is centered in the die opening. Finish screwing on the cap (**A**).

7. Holding the cap end of the extruder over the work surface, rotate the handle to force out a diamond-shaped tube of metal clay, about 1" (25 mm) long.

8. Working carefully with the tissue blade, slice off the tube at the opening in the end of the extruder. Slice carefully so as not to collapse the tube. Straighten the shape if necessary (**B**). Set the tube aside to air-dry or place it on the mug warmer. As it's drying, check it for warping and correct as needed.

9. Disassemble the extruder and remove any remaining fresh clay with a fine needle and small shaper so that it doesn't dry out. Combine the clay you removed with the metal clay stored in the package.

Making the Bead without an Extruder

If you don't have a Makin's Ultimate Clay Extruder, you can make Tubular Bead #2 with this alternative method. You'll need a plastic drinking straw and a wooden toothpick.

1. Oil the inside of the straw. Roll the lump of metal clay into a rope 1" (2.5 cm) long and press it into the drinking straw. It should fit the straw snugly.

2. Oil the toothpick and push it all the way through the metal clay. Set the straw aside to let the metal clay air-dry (which will take a while). Do not dry on the mug warmer.

3. When the metal clay is completely dry, slide the toothpick and metal clay bead out of the straw.

4. Use a coarse salon board to sand along the length of the bead to made a diamond-shaped cross section.

5. Remove the toothpick from the bead. If the toothpick is not loose enough to slip out of the bead, snip off the protruding ends, level with the ends of the bead, and sand them flat.

6. Roll out a ball of metal clay about ½" (13 mm) in diameter to form a sheet that is six cards thick. Cut two holes in the sheet with the small cutter, spacing them about 1" (25 mm apart).

7. Use a tissue blade to cut two diamond shapes around the holes you cut in step 6. These shapes will be the bead caps and should be larger than the ends of the bead. Set aside to dry.

8. Continue with the project instructions for Making the Domed Caps, page 77.

9. Follow steps 3 and 4 in Making the Spiral Coil, page 77, skipping steps 1, 2, and 5.

10. Roll out a long thin coil of metal clay on the oiled work surface and follow steps 6–8. Then continue with the rest of the instructions for this bead.

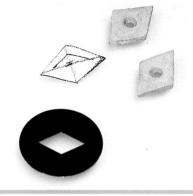

C. Make a template for the diamond caps by tracing around the diamond-shaped die.

MAKING THE DIAMOND-SHAPED CAPS

1. While the metal clay tube is drying, lightly oil the work surface and the roller.

2. Place the diamond-shaped die on a piece of paper. Trace around the diamond shape with a pencil. Remove the die and draw a line ⅛" (3mm) around the perimeter of the first drawing. Cut out the larger diamond shape, which will be your template for the caps (**C**). (If you don't have the extruder die, simply draw a diamond shape whose perimeter is ⅛" (3mm) larger than the outside diameter of the body of your bead.)

3. Roll a small lump of PMC into a ball about ½" (13 mm) in diameter. Place it on your work surface and flatten it slightly with your finger.

4. Place a six-card stack of playing cards on each side of the flattened lump. Roll the lump into a sheet, level with the height of the cards.

5. Cut two holes in the sheet, about 1" (25 mm) apart, with the small clay cutter.

6. Place the diamond pattern on the metal clay sheet, centering it on one of the holes. Work carefully with the tissue blade to cut out the diamond shape from the sheet. Repeat to make a second diamond shape.

7. Place both shapes on the mug warmer to dry completely. Then sand and refine their edges. Sand them so that they lie flat.

MAKING THE DOMED CAPS

1. Form the polymer clay into two small mounds. These mounds will support the marbles or beads, so be sure to make them large enough. Place them on the playing card.

2. Press one marble or bead into each polymer clay mound, so that about three-quarters of each sphere protrudes above the surface. Lightly oil the protruding surface.

3. Lightly oil the roller and the work surface. Roll a small lump of PMC into a ball about ¼" (6 mm) in diameter. Place it on the work surface and flatten it slightly with your finger. Place a three-card stack of playing cards on either side of the flattened lump. With the roller, roll the lump into a sheet, level with the height of the cards.

4. With the small clay cutter or tubing, punch two holes in the sheet, no less than 1" (2.5 cm) apart. Cut another circle in the sheet with the large clay cutter, centering it over one small hole

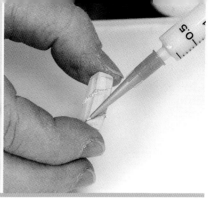

D. As the metal clay circles dry, they conform to the shape of the polymer supports to form the domed caps.

E. Apply slip along the moistened pencil line.

to make a flattened doughnut. Repeat to make a second doughnut.

5. Working carefully with the tissue blade, remove the excess clay around the doughnuts. Remove the metal clay from the small hole with the needle tool or scribe. Lift the doughnuts off the work surface and drape them on the supporter marbles or bead, pressing each one gently to conform to the spherical shape to form domes. Set the caps aside to air-dry **(D)**.

6. When both domed caps are partially dry (at the leather-hard stage), gently lift them off the spheres and place them on the mug warmer with the dome (convex) side down. Allow them to dry completely.

7. Return the polymer clay to its original packaging. Discard the playing card. (It now has a thin film of polymer clay, which you don't want to transfer to your metal clay. It would create unsafe fumes during firing.)

8. Place the dried dome caps, dome side up, on a salon board and very gently sand them until their bases are even and flat. Then sand around the edges so that they are slightly rounded, to create the illusion of an even greater slope.

Tip

To tell if a metal clay object is completely dry, put the object on a sheet of clean glass or mirror. After 15 to 20 seconds, lift the object from the surface. If the object is still not dry, there will be condensation on the glass surface. Let the object dry until it passes this condensation test.

MAKING THE SPIRAL COIL

1. Lightly oil the inside of the extruder and the circular die.

2. Place the die into the cap of the extruder and place a lump of PMC Standard, about ½" (13 mm) in diameter, in the extruder. Screw on the extruder cap. Stand the extruder on end on the worktable, resting on a piece of moist paper towel to keep the extruder from drying out.

3. Draw a spiral path along the length of the metal clay tube with a pencil. Moisten the pencil line with the filled waterbrush or wet paintbrush.

4. Push the narrow point onto the PMC syringe and push out slip along the moistened pencil line, depositing a little extra around each end of the tube **(E)**. It's easier to apply the slip by holding the syringe steady and rotating the tube. Wrap a moist piece of paper towel around the tip of the syringe and set it aside.

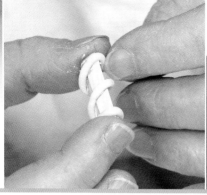
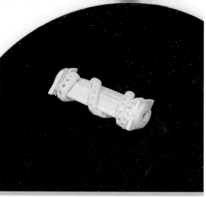

F. Extrude a length of metal clay to make the spiral coil.

G. Apply the spiral coil.

H. Join the diamond and dome caps to the tube, one at each end.

5. Holding the bottom cap end of the extruder over the work surface, rotate the extruder handle to form a long, snakelike coil of metal clay about 3" (7.5 cm) long **(F)**. Working quickly, slice the metal clay off the extruder with the tissue blade and set the extruder aside on the moist paper towel.

6. Wrap the coil around the tube, following the path of the slip. Wrap a little extra around each end of the tube, leaving a small "tail" extending slightly past each end **(G)**.

7. With the point of the pencil, make equally spaced depressions along the spiral coil, pressing gently to secure it to the surface of the tube as you decorate it.

8. Set the bead on the mug warmer to dry completely. Then sand each end of the tube so that they are flat and parallel to each other. Check to be sure the coil has a secure join. Fill any gaps with fresh slip and dry it again.

JOINING THE TUBE AND CAPS

1. Moisten the surface of one of the diamond shapes and the edge of one of the domed caps. Then apply slip to the edge of the dome with the syringe.

2. Press the domed cap gently onto the diamond shape and rotate it to join them firmly. Set the joined caps aside on a mug warmer to dry. Then carefully pop off any excess slip with the art knife. You can reconstitute this dried slip with water to make homemade slip.

3. Repeat steps 1 and 2 with the remaining diamond and dome caps.

4. When the two cap units are completely dry, check to make sure that there are no gaps in the joint. If needed, fill gaps with slip and let dry again. Make sure that the undersides of the diamond shapes are flat. If not, sand again.

5. Moisten the flat surface of one of the diamond shapes and one end of the tube.

6. With the syringe, apply slip to one end of the tube and press one cap unit onto it.

7. Repeat steps 4–6, joining the remaining cap unit to the other end of the tube.

8. Set the tube aside to dry on the mug warmer **(H)**. Then remove all excess slip, if any, with the art knife. Clean up any areas of the tube that need it, using salon boards or emery paper. Fill any gaps with fresh slip. Moisten areas before smoothing them, if needed, and then dry again.

Tip

The small tips that florists use to hold water for a single flower make good caps for the PMC syringe, helping to keep the slip from drying out. Fill one with water and push in the stringe tip.

Pan's Dream

ARTIST: Catherine Davies Paetz
MATERIAL: fine and sterling silver, 24k gold, hematite
TECHNIQUES: extruded tubes, keum-boo (Korean gold-foil bonding technique
DIMENSIONS: longest bead 1⅛" high × 3/16" diameter (30 mm × 5 mm), overall width 3½" (9 cm)

FIRING THE TUBULAR BEAD #2

1. Place the Kaowool firing pad on the firing surface, kiln pad, or firebrick in a cold kiln.

2. Place the bead on the firing pad and close the kiln door.

3. Turn on the kiln and select the program that will allow the kiln to run for 2 hours at 1650°F (900°C). Although PMC3 slip can be fired at lower temperatures, this bead must be fired at a higher temperature because the main body of the bead is made of PMC Standard.

4. After the kiln has completed the firing cycle, allow it to cool down a little. Then open the door to allow it to cool down even more.

5. Check the digital readout of the temperature on the kiln and, after the kiln has cooled down, put on the heavy gloves and move the bead with tweezers either to another fireproof surface to air-cool or into a large stainless-steel bowl filled with cool water to quench it.

6. Finish and polish bead (see page 25).

photo: Catherine Davies Paetz

Winged Hollow BEAD

"A bead with wings takes flight."

This Hollow Bead

takes flight with thin extensions—"wings" joined to the body of the bead. The wings are textured with rubber stamps. After being formed and textured, they are applied on end (perpendicular) to the surface of the bead. The hollow bead body is made by wrapping metal clay around a gemstone bead, which serves as an armature, or support, during the construction and drying processes. When the metal clay has partially dried, the bead body is removed from the gemstone bead by cutting the body into two equal parts, or hemispheres. The hemispheres are then reconnected at the equator to form a completely spherical, hollow bead. This bead-making process is an adaptation of a much-appreciated concept developed by J. Fred Woell.

What You Will Need

- 8–9 g of PMC+
- 1 container of PMC+ slip
- 1 large gemstone bead about ½" (12 mm) in diameter (or other smooth, nonporous, round object of similar size with a drilled central hole)
- 1 toothpick
- instant-bonding glue (such as Super Glue)
- 1 small bottle of olive oil (or other suitable lubricant)
- 1 piece of cellulose kitchen sponge, 1" (25 mm) square
- 1 porcelain or stainless-steel saucer or similar container (for the oiled sponge)
- 1 work surface (tempered glass or Plexiglas)
- 1 tissue blade
- 1 plastic roller
- 1 black lead pencil
- 2 three-card stacks of playing cards

- 1 brass clay cutter or short length of brass tubing, about ⅛" (3 mm) in diameter
- 1 brass clay cutter or short length of brass tubing, about ⅜" (10 mm) in diameter
- 1 mug warmer
- 1 circle template with graduated diameters
- 2 five-card stacks of playing cards
- 2 rubber stamps with shallow designs (identical or two different designs) (for textured wings, optional)
- 1 thin sewing needle
- salon boards in coarse and fine grits
- color or clay shapers
- 1 waterbrush (or small container of water and fine-tipped sable paintbrush)
- 1 pin vise (optional)

The finished Winged Hollow Bead on necklace of malachite beads, strung on hand-knotted silk.

"Drift, explore adjacencies, begin anywhere." Bruce Mau

A. Completely cover the gemstone bead with metal clay strips cut from a sheet rolled out to measure three playing cards thick.

B. Slice the PMC strip to form two hemispheres. Remember to move the sharp blade away from your fingers as you work.

C. Hold the toothpick and carefully remove the hemisphere opposite the toothpick.

- 1 art knife
  (X-Acto, for example)
- 1 small cup or scoop
- 1 small fireproof container
  (a terra-cotta flowerpot
  saucer or stainless-steel
  shallow bowl, for example)
- alumina hydrate (enough
  to fill the small fireproof
  container)
- 1 good-quality dust mask
  or respirator (for fine
  particulates)
- 1 pair vinyl gloves
- 1 PMC kiln
- 1 fireproof surface for
  the kiln with good, active
  ventilation
- 1 firing surface, kiln pad, or
  firebrick
- 1 pair long barbecue tongs
- 1 barbecue spatula
- 1 pair extra-heavy leather
  work gloves or potter's
  gloves (fire retardant)
- 1 large stainless-steel bowl
  filled with cool water
- 1 pair long steel tweezers

MAKING THE HEMISPHERES

1. Insert a toothpick in one hole of the gemstone bead. If the toothpick isn't secure, add a little instant-bonding glue to the opening and reinsert it.

2. Oil the work surface, roller, the gemstone bead, and your hands.

3. Roll a small lump of PMC into a ball about ½" (12 mm) in diameter. Place the ball on your work surface and flatten it slightly with your finger.

4. Place the three-card stack of playing cards on either side of the flattened lump. With the roller, roll the lump into a sheet, level with height of the cards.

5. Trim a strip to fit around the large gemstone bead. It should be wide enough to extend beyond the bead.

6. Wrap the strip around the bead, smoothing seams and bumps. Trim extra material. Gently press the metal clay to conform to the surface.

7. Completely cover the bead, using additional clay if needed (**A**).

8. Cut a small hole opposite the toothpick hole with the ⅛" (3 mm)-diameter brass tubing or clay cutter.

9. Set the bead aside to dry to a partially dry, leather-hard state. Then draw a light pencil line around the "equator" (circumference) of the bead.

10. With the tissue blade or art knife, slice along the line, cutting the sphere about in half (**B**).

11. Gently remove the hemisphere opposite the toothpick (**C**). Set it aside on the mug warmer, convex side up, and allow it to dry completely.

12. Rotating the toothpick slightly as you work, carefully slide the other hemisphere off the bead, past the toothpick.

13. Place this hemisphere on the work surface, concave side up. With the same cutter you used in step 8, cut a hole around the hole that the toothpick made, pressing the cutter into the partially dry clay until it cuts through to the work surface.

14. Place the two bowl-shaped forms on the heated mug warmer, convex sides up. Turn them several times, finishing with convex sides up, until they're completely dry.

MAKING THE HOLE SUPPORTS

1. Roll a small lump of PMC into a ball about ¼" (6 mm) in diameter. Place it on your work surface and flatten it slightly with your finger.

2. Place the three-card stack of playing cards on either side of the flattened lump. With the roller, roll the lump into a sheet, level with height of the cards.

3. Cut two circles in the metal clay sheet with the ⅛" (3 mm) -diameter brass tubing or clay cutter, spacing them at least 1" (25 mm) apart. Do not remove the metal clay sheet from the work surface.

4. Cut two more circles in the sheet with the ⅜" (10 mm) -diameter tubing or cutter, centering each one around the smaller circle, to make two flattened doughnut shapes.

5. Working carefully with the tissue blade, lift each hole support off the work surface and place one on each of the hemispheres on the mug warmer. The supports won't stick, but adjust them to fit the curve of the hemispheres so they are shaped as they dry.

MAKING THE WINGS

1. On the circle template, locate a circle with a slightly larger diameter than the gemstone bead that you used to form the hemispheres.

2. After taping the dull edge of the tissue blade for visibility, carefully and lightly lubricate the sharp edge and then your hands with the olive oil and sponge. (You might also need to relubricate the work surface, the roller, and your hands if it feels like they've lost oil with use.)

3. Roll a lump of PMC+ into a ball, about ½" (13 mm) in diameter.

4. To make wings with texture, place the lump of metal clay on one of the rubber stamps and flatten it slightly with the palm of your hand. Place a five-card stack of playing cards on either side of the flattened lump. With the roller, roll the lump into a sheet, level with height of the cards. Do not remove the metal clay sheet from the stamp. (To make wings without texture, just roll out metal clay sheet to five cards thick and skip ahead to step 7.)

5. Place the second rubber stamp on top of the metal clay sheet. With the roller, press the second stamp into the metal clay sheet. Do not press too hard or you will thin the metal clay sheet—apply just enough pressure to transfer the design on the stamp to the metal clay. Lift the stamp.

6. Remove the metal clay sheet from the rubber stamp it is resting on.

7. Place the metal clay sheet on the work surface.

Tip

If you can't rest the card stacks directly on the rubber stamp, place them on each side of the stamp and add extra cards to lift the five-card stack to the right height.

8. Place the circle template on the metal clay sheet, positioning the circle with the diameter you selected directly over the sheet.

9. With the sewing needle, draw that circle into the metal clay.

10. Using the circle template markings as a registration mark, make four very tiny marks at the edge of the drawn circle with the needle: one at top, one at bottom, and one mark on each side, dividing the circle into equal quarters (D).

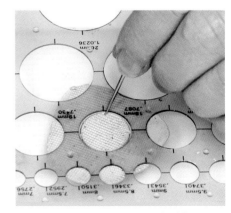

D. Make tiny needle marks at each of the cardinal points of the circle, as if points on a compass: north, south, east, and west.

E. With the tissue blade, cut a straight line through two marked points on the circles to make two semicircles.

F. Trim the semicircle strips, angling the ends.

11. Now select a circle on the template that is about ¼" (6 mm) larger than the first circle you selected. Lay the template on the metal clay sheet with the second circle positioned over the first. Align the registration marks with the markings on the new template circle. Draw around the second circle with the needle. You will have two concentric circles.

12. Line up the tissue blade with the registration marks at the north and south positions of the circles. Carefully cut a straight line through the diameters of both circles to form two semicircle strips (**E**).

13. Working carefully with the tissue blade, lift out the center circle and the outer excess metal clay sheet and return them to the package or plastic wrap.

14. Carefully trim the ends of each of the semicircle strips at an angle, beginning a short distance away from one end and angling the cut. Be sure the strips are long enough to span the two hole supports on the bead. You can always trim away more later if necessary (**F**).

15. Lift each of the semicircle strips off the rubber stamp and set them aside to dry on the mug warmer. Return all metal clay trimmings to the package or plastic wrap.

16. Repeat steps 3–15. You will now have four trimmed semicircular strips.

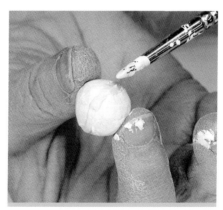

G. Apply a generous amount of slip to the joint of the hemispheres.

JOINING THE HEMISPHERES

1. When the hemispheres are completely dry, place one on the gemstone support. Refine the outsides of the hemisphere by sanding or wetting lightly and smoothing with the shaper—or both. If the shrinkage prevents you from being able to reinsert the gemstone bead, carefully set the hemisphere on your finger as you sand and refine. Repeat the process to sand and refine the second hemisphere.

2. Refine the sliced edge of each hemisphere by sanding it with a salon board. The edges of the two hemispheres should be flat and should meet evenly. Be sure to keep the hemispheres the same size and the bottom edges of each hemisphere of equal diameters.

3. With the filled waterbrush or wet paintbrush, moisten the edge of each hemisphere. Add PMC+ slip to each edge with the shaper.

4. Join the hemisphere edges, pressing and rotating them slightly to form a sphere. Add extra PMC+ slip on the outside of the joint (**G**).

5. Set the joined sphere aside to dry completely. Then sand and refine the surfaces. Check to make certain that the joint is secure. Where needed, fill any gaps with PMC+ slip. Work carefully—remember, in this greenware (unfired) state, the sphere is somewhat fragile.

ADDING THE HOLE SUPPORTS

1. When the sphere and hole supports are dry, with the filled waterbrush or wet paintbrush, moisten the concave side of one of the supports and the area around one of the holes in the sphere.

2. Use the shaper to add PMC+ slip to the moistened area on the sphere. Gently press the hole support onto the slipped area, matching the hole in the support to the hole in the sphere. Rotate the support a little to secure the joint and adjust the fit.

3. Repeat steps 1 and 2 for the second hole support.

Tip

To protect your hands from heat while using the hair dryer, make a support for the sphere. Insert a needle into a pin vise and slide the needle through the holes in the sphere. Hold the needle horizontally and the sphere will stay in place as you direct the hot air around it with the dryer.

ADDING THE WINGS

1. Remove the semicircular strips (the wings) from the mug warmer. Repair any flaws by sanding or adding slip, if needed, and refine the edges. Handle the pieces carefully as they are fragile in this greenware state.

2. Hold a wing to the surface of the sphere, with each end of the semicircle at the hole supports and with the smaller curve of the wing resting on the sphere surface. Adjust the fit either with salon boards or with the art knife.

3. Lightly moisten the smaller curve of the wing and the area on the sphere where you'll position it. Add PMC+ slip to the moistened area of the sphere. Press the wing into the slip, carefully, but firmly, to secure it **(H)**.

4. Hold the wing in place on the sphere for about 30 seconds. Then begin the drying process with the hair dryer. After a minute or two, place the sphere directly on the mug warmer.

5. Repeat steps 2–4 with each of the remaining three wings, spacing them evenly around the sphere.

6. When the wing joints are completely dry, remove all the excess slip with the art knife. Handle the wings carefully—they're quite fragile.

7. Refine the edges of the wings with salon boards. Repair any flaws with fresh slip. Dry the bead again. Clean up any excess slip on the bead.

8. With the shaper and the filled waterbrush or wet paintbrush, smooth the surfaces of the bead. Allow it to dry thoroughly.

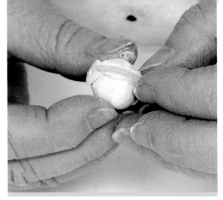

H. Press the shaped curve of the wing onto the curved surface of the sphere where it will rest.

FIRING THE BEAD

1. Put on the respirator or dust mask and vinyl gloves. Fill the small fireproof container with alumina hydrate.

2. Place the bead on the alumina hydrate. Then place the container on a firing surface, kiln pad, or firebrick in a cold kiln. Close the kiln door.

3. Turn on the kiln and select the program that will allow the kiln to run for 2 hours at 1650°F (900°C).

4. After the kiln has completed the firing cycle, allow it to cool down a little. Then open the door to allow it to cool down even more.

5. Check the digital readout of the temperature on the kiln and, after the kiln has cooled down, put on the heavy gloves and move the bead with tweezers either to another fireproof surface to air-cool or into a large stainless-steel bowl filled with cool water to quench it.

6. Finish and polish bead (see page 25).

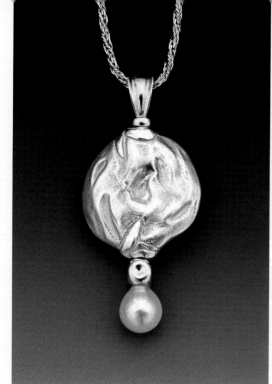

photo: Frank Poole

Sculpted Bead Pendant

ARTIST: Nancy Karpel

MATERIALS: fine silver, 14k gold, pearl

TECHNIQUES: metal clay, hollow core construction (wax)

DIMENSIONS: central bead $7/8$" high × $3/4$" wide × $1/4$" deep (21 mm × 19 mm × 5 mm)

Beads

ARTIST: Barbara Briggs

MATERIALS: fine silver and sterling silver, 24k gold

TECHNIQUES: hollow core construction (cork clay), metal clay, paste-painting, tumbling, polishing, patination

DIMENSIONS: round $7/8$" (20 mm), oval $1\,1/4$" × $7/8$" (30 mm × 20 mm)

photo: Barbara Briggs

Lantern BEAD

SKILL LEVEL: Intermediate to advanced
FINISHED SIZE: ¾" diameter × 1¾" wide
(20 mm × 45 mm)

"The Lantern Bead combines slip-painting and paper folding."

What You Will Need

- 4–5 g of PMC3
- 1 container (or more) of PMC slip
- 1 sheet of 220-grit wet/dry emery paper
- 1 sharp steel scribe or large sewing needle
- 1 ruler
- 1 pair scissors
- rubber cement or another type of contact cement or glue
- 1 small art paintbrush
- 1 color or clay shaper
- a few drops of water, to thin the slip (use distilled if hard)
- 1 mug warmer
- 1 piece of copper mesh screen, 3" (7.5 cm) square
- assorted salon boards in grits from coarse to fine
- 1 art knife (X-Acto, for example)

- 1 small bottle of olive oil (or other suitable lubricant)
- 1 piece of cellulose kitchen sponge, 1" (25 mm) square
- 1 porcelain or stainless-steel saucer or similar container (for the oiled sponge)
- 1 work surface (tempered glass or Plexiglas)
- 1 plastic roller
- 2 four-card stacks of playing cards
- 1 brass clay cutter or short length of brass tubing, about ¼" (6 mm) in diameter
- 1 brass clay cutter or short length of brass tubing, about ⅝" (16 mm) in diameter
- 1 jeweler's or leather-design stamping punch or letterpress ornament
- 1 pair small, fine-pointed tweezers

The finished Lantern Bead on a necklace of disk-shaped bone beads, strung on hand-knotted silk.

"Someday soon it will realized that the artist is the leader of humankind on the path to absolute truth." Alfred Adler

The Lantern Bead

is based on a paper project I made in elementary school. The paper is cut, glued, and folded to resemble a lantern. You can expand this simple concept to create intricate origami forms. Slip-painting folded paper is an idea developed by Zahava Lambert.

You'll form the lantern shape with emery paper, for three reasons. First, emery paper forms stiff, crisp folds. Second, it won't absorb the water from the slip-painting, which would distort the form. Third, emery paper gives the inside of the bead a slight texture. The Lantern Bead is embellished with small metal clay granules. The instructions call for at least eight, but make more if that seems a good design decision for your bead. For finishing, you'll need a tumbler. The steel shot gets inside the bead and cleans and burnishes the surface more easily than hand burnishing would.

A. Draw a line with the scribe on each of the short ends of the emery-paper square.

B. Draw equidistant lines between the two original lines, along the long edge of the rectangle.

C. Working with the scribe marks as a guide, cut a series of slits in the folded emery-paper rectangle.

- 1 waterbrush (or small container of water and fine-tipped sable paintbrush)
- 1 PMC kiln
- 1 fireproof surface for the kiln with good, active ventilation
- 1 small cup or scoop
- 1 small fireproof container (a terra-cotta flowerpot saucer or stainless-steel shallow bowl, for example)
- alumina hydrate (enough to fill the fireproof container)
- good-quality dust mask or respirator (for fine particulates)
- 1 pair vinyl gloves
- 1 firing surface, kiln pad, or firebrick
- 1 pair long barbecue tongs
- 1 barbecue spatula
- 1 pair extra-heavy leather work gloves or potter's gloves (fire retardant)
- 1 large stainless-steel bowl filled with cool water
- 1 pair long steel tweezers

MAKING THE PAPER FORM

1. Cut a piece of the emery paper into a small rectangle that measures about 2" × 1⅝" (5 cm × 4 cm).

2. With the scribe, draw a line about 5/16" (8 mm) in from each of the shorter ends. Don't scratch too hard—just enough to mark the line **(A)**.

3. Again working with the scribe, draw six evenly spaced parallel lines between the lines you drew in step 2—about ¼" (6 mm) apart and parallel to the long edge of the rectangle **(B)**.

4. With the grit side of the emery paper up, align the two short edges to fold the rectangle in half. Lightly crease the fold several times with your fingernail.

5. With scissors, cut slits along the lines you drew in steps 2 and 3 **(C)**.

6. Open the folded rectangle. You'll have seven cut strips in the emery paper.

7. Turn on the active ventilation. Apply a thin layer of rubber cement along the length (long side) of one of the end strips, on the paper side of the emery paper. Then apply a thin layer of cement on the other end strip, on the grit side of the emery paper.

8. Allow the rubber cement to dry a little until it's slightly tacky.

9. Press the two end strips together, with one finger on the inside of the tube that forms. Try to keep the tube round.

10. When the cement is thoroughly dry and the ends hold together on their own, press the other ends of the tube toward each other, compressing the fold and allowing the strips to bow outward **(D)**. The bead shape varies depending on how much the fold is compressed. Be careful not to bend and rebend the paper, or it will split.

D. Glue together the long sides of the paper. Bend the fold to create the lantern shape.

E. Only the first layer of slip is thinned with water. Avoid painting the inside of the paper form. If slip gets inside, remove as much as possible while still wet with a scribe or sewing needle, or it will leave unsightly lumps or bumps.

F. After the slip-painted lantern form is completely dry, refine the ends with salon boards and the art knife.

SLIP-PAINTING

1. With the shaper, scoop about ½ teaspoon of PMC3 slip onto your work surface.

2. Add a small drop of water to the slip and stir with the shaper until well combined. You'll only need thinned slip for the first two layers of the lantern.

3. Holding one end of the lantern, apply a layer of the thinned PMC3 slip to the surface with the paintbrush. Leave a small portion of one end unpainted so you have an area to hold onto (**E**).

Tip

If you prefer to thin the slip for every layer you paint onto your lantern, paint at least ten layers and no more than twelve. Remember, the thicker the slip, the more lumps and bumps you'll need to smooth away after you've applied the final layer.

4. Partially dry the lantern with a hair dryer, first mounting the form in a pair of cross-lock tweezers to protect your fingers from the heat. After the lantern is partially dry, remove it from the tweezers and paint the unpainted area.

5. Dry it completely on the mug warmer, standing the form vertically, with the partially dried end down.

6. Repeat steps 3–5 another ten to twelve times (if you are applying layers of thinned slip) or eight times (if you are applying layers of unthinned slip). After the first layer, you can paint the entire surface of the lantern by holding the open ends with your fingers. Each time you add a new layer, add a little extra slip to the folds to strengthen the form. Add slip to the seam, too, filling in any gaps. Add enough layers to make a metal clay skin three to five playing cards thick. (Slip thickness can vary, so keep in mind how thick the form needs to be, while you also keep track of the number of layers you are adding.) Dry each layer before applying the next layer of slip.

7. When the form is completely dry, check for cracks or other flaws and add more slip to repair them. If there are small bumps, you can remove them in one of three ways: Moisten them a little with water, smooth them with the shaper, and let dry; simply sand them off with salon boards or emery paper; or scrape them gently with an art knife (**F**).

8. Very lightly moisten the edges of one of the openings in the lantern with the filled waterbrush or wet paintbrush. Gently slice away any bumps along those edges with the art knife or X-Acto knife. Repeat for the other edge and the edges of the slits.

9. Peek inside the bead and carefully scrape away any drips you see with the needle, scribe, or art knife.

10. Allow the lantern to dry completely. Then sand and refine the ends with the salon boards. (Do not save this sanding dust for reconstituted slip, because there may be emery paper dust in it. Instead, save it separately for refining.

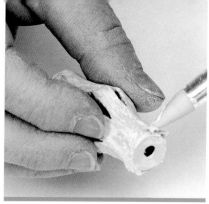

G. The end caps are secured to each end of the lantern with water and slip.

MAKING THE END CAPS

1. After taping the dull edge of the tissue blade for visibility, carefully and lightly lubricate the sharp edge and then your hands with the olive oil and the sponge. Lightly oil the work surface, the roller, and the pencil.

2. Roll a small lump of PMC3 into a ball about ½" (13 mm) in diameter. Place it on the work surface and flatten it slightly with your finger.

3. Place a four-card stack of playing cards on either side of the flattened lump. With the roller, roll the lump into a sheet, level with height of the cards.

4. Cut two holes in the sheet with the small brass tubing or circle-shaped clay cutter, spacing them about 1" (2.5 cm) apart.

5. To complete the end caps, cut two circles in the sheet with the large tubing or cutter, centering each one around the smaller circles. The large circles should have a larger diameter than the openings at each end of the lantern.

6. Working carefully with the tissue blade, lift the end caps from the work surface and set them on the mug warmer to dry.

MAKING THE GRANULES

1. Oil the work surface, the roller, the brass tubing or clay cutter, and your hands.

2. Roll a lump of PMC+ into a ball about 1" (2.5 cm) in diameter.

3. With the palm of your hand, flatten the ball on the work surface. Place one three-card stack of playing cards on each side of the flattened lump. With the roller, roll the metal clay into a sheet, level with height of the cards. Leave the metal clay on the work surface.

4. Cut at least eight circles in the metal sheet with the tubing or cutter. These circles will make granules of equal size. (Cut extra circles if you want to make more granules for this project or future projects.)

5. Roll the circles into small spheres and place them back on the work surface.

6. With the punch or letterpress ornament, gently press the design into each of the spheres, compressing and flattening them.

7. Working carefully with the tissue blade, lift the granules off the work surface and place them on the mug warmer to dry.

JOINING THE LANTERN, END CAPS, AND GRANULES

1. When the lantern, end caps, and granules are all completely dry, remove them from the mug warmer with tweezers (remember, they're hot).

2. Check for any flaws in the pieces and repair them. Sand the edges and surfaces of the end caps and sand the backs of each of the granules so they are completely flat.

3. With the filled waterbrush or a wet paintbrush, moisten one side of one end cap and the edges at one end of the lantern. With the shaper, add a substantial amount of slip to the moist side of the end cap.

4. Press the slipped side of the end cap onto the moistened end of the lantern. Rotate to secure the joint, making sure the cap is centered over the opening in the end of the lantern. Partially dry this end of the lantern on the mug warmer. Do not remove the excess slip (**G**).

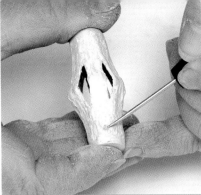

H. The unfired metal clay is reactivated with a drop of water.

I. The first granule is placed at the end of the lantern bead, near the end caps.

5. Repeat steps 3 and 4 to join the second end cap to the other end of the lantern.

6. Place the lantern bead on the mug warmer to dry completely.

7. Sand around the edges of the end cap with a salon board until it is even with the surface of the lantern bead.

8. With the filled waterbrush or wet paintbrush, apply one drop of water on the uncut, smooth surface near the end opening of the lantern bead. Let the metal clay absorb the water. Then rough up the area with the scribe or needle, to create a gooey, viscous spot on the bead. (Don't scrape so deeply you reach the surface of the emery paper.) This sticky surface will help the granule adhere to the bead (**H**).

9. With the shaper, add a generous amount of PMC3 slip to the moistened spot. Pick up one of the granules with the tweezer and place it on the slip. Gently press and rotate the granule with your finger to seat it securely at that spot (**I**).

10. Dry the granule joint completely. With the art knife, pop or slice off any excess slip around the granule.

11. Repeat steps 8–10 to position the remaining seven granules, so that you have four evenly spaced granules around each end of the bead.

12. Sand and refine the surface of the bead with salon boards or emery paper.

FIRING THE LANTERN BEAD

1. Put on the respirator or dust mask and the vinyl gloves. Fill the small fireproof container with alumina hydrate.

2. Place the bead on the alumina hydrate. Then place the container on a firing surface, kiln pad, or firebrick in a cold kiln. Close the kiln door.

3. Turn on the kiln on and select the program that will allow the kiln to run for 2 hours at 1650°F (900°C).

4. After the kiln has completed the firing cycle, allow it to cool down a little. Then open the door to allow it to cool down even more.

5. Check the digital readout of the temperature on the kiln and, after the kiln has cooled down, put on the heavy gloves and move the bead with tweezers either to another fireproof surface to air-cool or into a large stainless-steel bowl filled with cool water to quench it.

6. Finish and polish bead (see page 25).

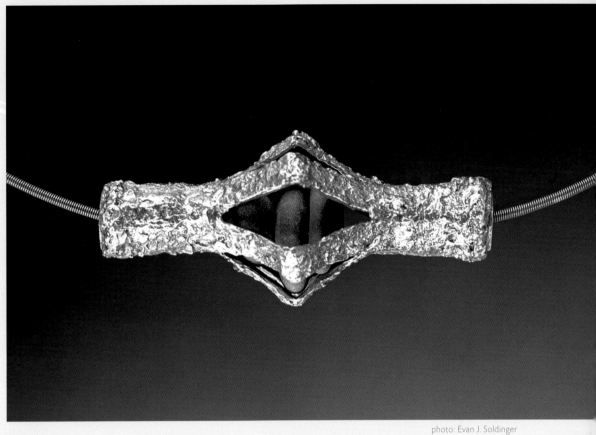

photo: Evan J. Soldinger

Lantern Bead

ARTIST: Linda Kaye-Moses

MATERIALS: fine and sterling silver, beach stones

TECHNIQUES: metal clay, patination

DIMENSIONS: 2½" wide × 1" diameter (63 mm × 25 mm)

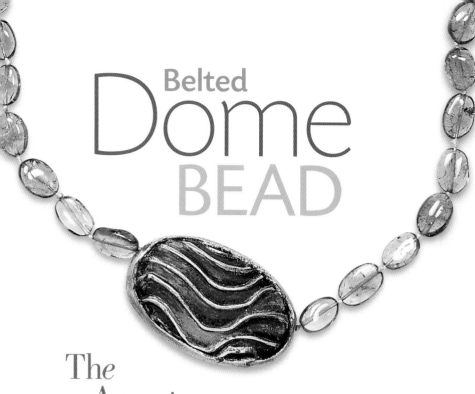

Belted
Dome
BEAD

SKILL LEVEL: Intermediate to advanced
FINISHED SIZE: 1" high × 1½" wide × ¼" deep
(25 mm × 38 mm × 6 mm)

"Hollow and brightly colored is this domed bead."

What You Will Need

- 18–20 g of PMC3
- 1 syringe of PMC3 slip
- 1 small ovoid stone, about 1½" × 3¾" × ½" thick (38 mm × 95 mm × 13 mm), or ready-made form of papier-mâché (such as Celluclay) of similar size
- 1 extra-fine black permanent marker
- 1 small bottle of olive oil (or other suitable lubricant)
- 1 piece of cellulose kitchen sponge, 1" (25 mm) square
- 1 porcelain or stainless-steel saucer or similar container (for the oiled sponge)
- 1 printing plate (as for the Draped Bead, page 63)
- 1 work surface (tempered glass or Plexiglas)
- 1 tissue blade
- 1 plastic roller
- 2 five-card stacks of playing cards
- 2 four-card stacks of playing cards
- 1 pair scissors
- 1 mug warmer

- 1 sheet of wet/dry emery paper, 400 grit
- 1 waterbrush (or small container of water and fine-tipped sable paintbrush)
- 1 color shaper or clay shaper
- 1 art knife (X-Acto, for example)
- salon boards, fine and coarse grit, or wet/dry emery paper, 220 and 600 grit
- 1 small, dry, flat paintbrush
- 1 black lead pencil
- 1 steel drill bit, size #46–50 (with pin vise to hold drill bit, optional)
- 1 PMC kiln
- 1 fireproof surface for the kiln with good, active ventilation
- 1 small cup or scoop
- 1 small fireproof container (a terra-cotta flowerpot saucer or shallow stainless-steel bowl, for example)
- alumina hydrate (enough to fill small fireproof container)

The
Armature for this hollow metal clay

bead is an ovoid (three-dimensional oval) stone that has been smoothed by tumbling in the river or sea. You may have, like me, collected some, but you can also find similar stones at gardening supply stores. Or you can make the armature from other materials, such as polymer clay (following manufacturer's instructions) or papier-mâché (as described in the sidebar on page 94).

You'll texture the bead with the printing plate you made for the Draped Bead (see page 63). The patterns will be unique because of the difference in the shape. The bead's surface colors are made with colored pencils, with fixative applied between the many layers. There's a final protective coating of microcrystalline wax.

The finished Belted Dome Bead on necklace of citrine beads, strung on hand-knotted silk.

"Drift. Explore adjacencies. Begin anywhere." Bruce Mau

- 1 respirator or good dust mask
- 1 pair vinyl gloves
- 1 firing surface, kiln pad, or firebrick
- 1 pair long barbecue tongs
- 1 barbecue spatula
- 1 pair extra-heavy leather work gloves or potter's gloves (fire retardant)
- 1 large stainless-steel bowl filled with cool water
- 1 pair long steel tweezers
- 1 jeweler's brass brush
- liquid dishwashing detergent
- assorted Tri-M-Ite polishing sheets
- 1 fine-tip paintbrush
- 1 jar of acrylic white gesso
- 1 paper cup
- 1 hair dryer
- 1 toothpick, skewer, or knitting needle, depending on the size of the bead hole
- 1 set of Prismacolor (not watercolor) pencils
- 1 pencil sharpener
- 1 can of matte Prismacolor fixative
- 1 jar of microcrystalline wax (such as Renaissance Wax)
- 5–10 small cotton swabs (like Q-Tips)
- 1 polishing cloth (such as a Sunshine cloth)
- 1 small chunk of liver of sulfur (about the size of a green pea)
- 1 white 100% cotton dress glove or other 100% cotton cloth
- fine-grade pumice powder

A. Work with scissors to trim the draped metal clay to hang slightly beyond the "equator" of the armature.

MAKING THE DOMES

1. With the black marker, mark a dot on one side of the stone or papier-mâché armature. The dot will help you keep track of which side of the stone you're working on.

2. After taping the dull edge of the tissue blade for visibility, carefully and lightly lubricate the sharp edge and then your hands with the olive oil and the sponge. Lightly oil the work surface, printing plate, stone, and roller.

3. Roll a piece of PMC3 into a ball, about ½" (12 mm) in diameter.

4. Place one five-card stack of playing cards on the work surface on each side of the metal clay. With the roller, roll the metal clay into a sheet, level with height of the cards.

5. Working carefully with the tissue blade, lift the metal clay sheet off the work surface and lay it on the printing plate.

6. Place one four-card stack alongside the metal clay sheet on the printing plate. Very firmly roll the metal clay onto the printing plate so that is level with height of the cards. The metal clay sheet should now have a perimeter slightly larger than the outer edges of the armature.

7. Remove the PMC3 sheet from the printing plate and drape it on the unmarked side of the armature. The edges of the metal clay sheet should extend beyond the "equator" of the armature.

8. Use the scissors to trim the draped sheet so the sides hang a little more than halfway down the sides of the armature **(A)**. Don't stretch the metal around the curve, but make it conform to the shape of the armature. Trim the excess material, leaving a little extra to work with as you sand and refine later.

9. Set the draped armature on a mug warmer, armature side down. Let it dry for 30 to 60 seconds.

10. When the metal clay feels slightly dry and holds its shape, trim again, if necessary, to remove any material that overhangs the equator. Then remove the domed metal clay from the armature and trim further as needed. Set it back on the mug warmer—without the armature and concave side up—to dry completely.

11. Repeat steps 3–10 to make the second dome for the bead, but this time use the marked side of the armature to form the metal clay.

Making a Papier-Mâché Armature

WHAT YOU WILL NEED:

- 1 handful of ready-made papier-mâché (such as Celluclay), sold by the bag
- water
- waxed paper
- coarse-grit wet/dry emery paper white glue (such as Sobo)

1. Moisten a small handful of papier-mâché with just enough water for it to hold together in a lump. Don't make it soggy.

2. Shape the material into an ovoid having the approximate dimensions needed for the project. Set the form on a piece of waxed paper to dry. Flip it over occasionally to allow all the sides to dry. When it's completely dry, it will be hard.

3. Sand and smooth the form with the emery paper to refine the ovoid shape.

4. Coat the surface of the form very lightly with a little white glue. Set it aside on a piece of waxed paper to dry again. When it's completely dry, it's ready to use.

JOINING THE DOMES

1. When both domes are completely dry, place one of them on top of the emery paper on a flat surface. Gently move the dome lightly back and forth and around the paper to sand the edges. Brush away excess sanding dust from the domes with the dry paintbrush (**B**). Repeat to sand the second dome.

2. Without adding any tip to the syringe, extrude a line of PMC3 slip along the edge of one of the domes. Use more slip than you think you need. Add slip along the inside dome edge, too (**C**).

3. Gently press together the edges of the two domes, adjusting the fit as you press and allowing some of the slip to ooze out.

4. Set the hollow form on the mug warmer and let dry completely. When the slip is dry, carefully pop off any excess with the art knife.

5. Refine the joint with salon boards (progressing from coarse grits to finer grits). The form is still fragile, so work with a light and patient touch.

6. Don't worry about any minor openings in the joint—the belt will fill them—but repair any major gaps by moistening them and adding fresh PMC3. Let dry again and sand the joint.

B. When sanding the domes, do not exert too much downward pressure—the greenware (unfired) forms are somewhat fragile, and the metal clay could snap if you push too hard.

C. Apply slip to the edge of the dome with the syringe.

D. Overlap the ends of the belt and trim them with a beveled cut. Then apply slip and press the joint securely.

E. As the bit approaches the inside of the hollow bead, it may catch. If so, back it off by rotating it counterclockwise. Drill the hole again until the bit breaks cleanly through to the interior of the bead.

MAKING THE BELT

1. After taping the dull edge of the tissue blade for visibility, carefully and lightly lubricate the sharp edge. Then oil your hands, the work surface, printing plate, and roller.

2. Roll a lump of PMC3 into a long cigar shape.

3. Place one four-card stack of playing cards on each side of the work surface. With the roller, roll the metal clay into a sheet, level with height of the cards. The metal clay sheet should be longer than the circumference of the hollow bead at the joint, but does not need to be the exact length—you'll trim the strip you need later.

4. Working carefully with the tissue blade, cut the belt as one long strip, ¼" (6 mm) wide and the full length of the metal sheet. Use the tissue blade to lift the excess metal clay and return it to the package or plastic wrap.

5. Check the length of the belt by wrapping it loosely around the dome bead at the joint, overlapping the ends. Don't stretch the strip—it should fit slightly loosely, because as it dries, it will shrink, and if the fit is too tight, the metal clay could crack.

6. Remove the belt from the bead and extrude a line of PMC3 slip around the joint of the bead.

7. Rewrap the strip around the bead and slice through the overlapping ends with the tissue blade with a bevel (obliquely angled) cut (**D**).

8. Add a generous amount of slip to the ends and press them together, joining the ends of the belt. Gently press along the entire belt without stretching it, starting at the spot opposite the joint, adjusting it to fit and trimming, if necessary.

9. Set the bead on the mug warmer to dry completely. Then sand the joint and edges of the belt with the salon board or emery paper, rounding the edges. Carefully pop off any excess slip with the art knife, scribe, or needle.

10. With the filled waterbrush or wet paintbrush, moisten the rough areas and smooth them with the color or clay shaper. Let dry again.

DRILLING THE HOLE

1. To mark the spot for drilling the hole, make an X with the pencil at each end of the bead, centering the mark across the width of the belt. Because this is a large bead, make the mark slightly above an imaginary line drawn across the center of gravity or equator of the bead, so that the bead won't unexpectedly flip over when strung on a chain or strand.

2. With the filled waterbrush or wet paintbrush, apply a dot of water on one of the pencil marks. Scratch into the moistened spot with a scribe, bringing up a little slip from the surface and making a small depression, which will help guide the drill bit.

3. Press the handheld drill bit gently into the depression, rotating it slowly. If the bit doesn't seem to be cutting the material, rotate it both clockwise and counterclockwise, clearing out dried clay shards as the bit cuts (**E**).

Tip

If the bead hole you've drilled has ragged edges, moisten the tip of the shaper and rotate it in the hole until the opening edge is smooth. If the hole is too small, rotate the wet shaper in the hole until it is large enough. If the hole is much too small, drill it to size with a larger drill bit.

4. Continue pressing lightly, rotating the bit until it reaches the inside of the bead. Take your time and don't force the drill bit. The bead is fragile and hollow, so if you push the bit, the pressure may stress and crack the form.

5. Clean up any excess slip or flaws with an art knife, salon boards, or emery paper. Recheck for any gaps in any of the joints and fill them with slip. Dry again and sand to refine.

FIRING THE BEAD

1. Put on the respirator or dust mask and vinyl gloves. Fill the small fireproof container with alumina hydrate.

2. Place the bead on the alumina hydrate and then place the container on a kiln pad, firing surface, or firebrick in a cold kiln. Close the kiln door.

3. Turn on the kiln on and select the program that will allow the kiln to run for 2 hours at 1650°F (900°C).

4. After the kiln has completed the firing cycle, allow it to cool down a little. Then open the door to allow it to cool down even more.

5. Check the digital readout of the temperature on the kiln and, after the kiln has cooled down, put on the heavy gloves and move the bead with tweezers either to another fireproof surface to air-cool or into a large stainless-steel bowl filled with cool water to quench it.

6. Matte-white silver oxides were deposited on the surface of the bead during the firing process (see page 25). Remove the silver oxides on the high points of the bead with a brass brush, water, and liquid dishwashing detergent avoiding the recessed areas, if possible.

7. The belt and high points of the bead will not be colored, so use the Tri-M-Ite polishing sheets to begin to put a finish on them. (As an alternative, you could finish these surfaces with polishing disks and a flexible shaft machine, but the recessed parts of the bead should not be touched.)

8. If you are going to patinate the bead, wash the bead in warm water with a very little bit of dishwashing liquid. Rinse off the the soapy water. If you are not going to patinate the bead, skip to "Coloring the Bead."

PATINATING THE BEAD

1. Put on the vinyl gloves and turn on active ventilation. Make a patination solution with liver of sulfur and hot water (see page 148).

2. Place the bead in clean hot water in a nonreactive container (such as a stainless-steel or glass bowl) to warm it.

3. Remove the bead from the hot water and dip it in the patination solution, leaving it submerged for about 5 seconds.

4. Rinse the bead in fresh hot water and allow it to warm up again. Repeat steps 2 and 3 until you achieve the level of patination you want.

F. Thinned gesso creates a foundation for the color. Paint it into the bead indentations only.

G. Try out the pencils' colors first on a clean piece of white paper, shading them in layers over each other—this is the time to play. Then reproduce the effects you like by applying colors to the bead indentations.

COLORING THE BEAD

1. Put a small amount of the gesso in the paper cup. Stir in a very small amount of water. The consistency of the gesso should be about the thickness of heavy cream.

2. Paint the gesso into the indentations on the bead with the fine-tip paintbrush **(F)**. Carefully wipe any gesso from the raised areas of the bead with a cotton swap. Dry the first layer completely, either by air-drying or by using the hair dryer. Add another layer of gesso if the first layer seems too thin or if there are gaps where the metal shows through.

3. With the scribe or an art knife, carefully scrape off any dried gesso in areas other than the sections that will be colored.

4. Sharpen very fine points on the Prismacolor pencils in the colors that you've selected. Apply color to the indentations, one light layer of color at a time, shading the colors and/or applying different colors in each indentation. If some areas are hard to reach with the fine points, rub the sides of the pencil points on a piece of paper to make flattened chisel points to reach the recesses **(G)**.

5. Turn on the active ventilation.

6. Create a support for the bead by sliding the bead onto a toothpick, skewer, or a knitting needle—or whatever the size of the hole permits.

7. Hold the support in one hand and, following the manufacturer's instructions, apply a light mist of Prismacolor fixative on all colored sections of the bead. Don't try to spray just within the indentations—you'll remove excess fixative from the surface of the bead later.

8. Apply more layers of color, as many as it takes to achieve the color results you like. Spray on fixative after each layer of color, except the final one.

9. Working with cotton swabs, apply a layer of microcrystalline wax to the final layer of color, following the manufacturer's instructions.

FINISHING THE BEAD

1. Dip the cotton glove or cloth in olive oil, then sprinkle on a very small amount of the pumice powder. Wipe the belt and the high points of the bead with the cloth to remove the fixative and brighten the surface. The patination will frame the colored sections.

2. Wipe off any excess olive oil on the bead.

3. Brighten the belt and the high points of the bead by polishing those surfaces with the Tri-M-Ite sheets, progressing from medium coarseness to fine. Wipe the surfaces with the polishing cloth.

photo: Eleanor Moty

Necklace

ARTIST: Eleanor Moty

MATERIALS: fine silver, sterling silver, Picasso Jasper, pearls

TECHNIQUES: metal clay, hollow core construction (Sculptamold)

DIMENSIONS: PMC beads 1" × 1½" (2.5 cm × 3.8 cm), total length 17" (43 cm)

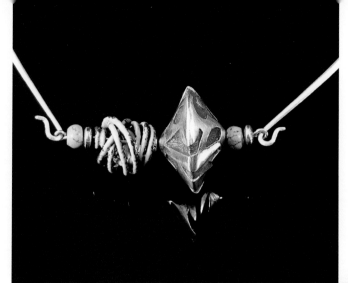

photo: Maggie Bergman

Bi-Cone Bead

ARTIST: Maggie Bergman

MATERIALS: fine and sterling silver PMC, colored pencil, copper, vitreous enamel, turquoise

TECHNIQUES: metal clay, dry construction (cork clay), water etching, colored pencil

DIMENSIONS: 1⅛" × ¾" (30 mm × 18 mm)

photo: Maggie Bergman

Floral Bead

ARTIST: Maggie Bergman

MATERIALS: fine silver, colored pencil

TECHNIQUES: metal clay, hollow core construction (cork clay), water etching, colored-pencil

DIMENSIONS: 2¼" × ⅝" (57 mm × 15 mm)

Two Beads

ARTIST: Hadar Jacobson

MATERIAL: fine silver

TECHNIQUES: metal clay, hollow core construction (rock and marble)

DIMENSIONS: sphere ¾" (20 mm) diameter, "rock" 1¾" × ¾" (45 mm × 20 mm)

photo: Hadar Jacobson

Enameled
Dome
BEAD

"Translucent enamel colors
add dimension to this
deeply domed bead."

This Large, Deeply

domed form has a flat back, a construction technique adapted from a concept developed and taught by Barbara Becker Simon. This project offers a brief introduction to enameling fine silver, a process of placing very finely ground particles of colored glass on metal and firing them until they fuse. This project's enameling method is an adaptation of traditional champlevé enameling, in which the background is etched to create "cells" that accept the enamels. This bead's cells are made by impressing a carved printing block into metal clay. The block is carved with a simple design specifically intended for wet inlay of vitreous enamels, with a different pattern on each side.

Usually enamels are finished to a glossy surface, but this project demonstrates a technique for achieving a matte finish, which gives the enamels a translucency similar to beach glass.

What You Will Need

- 18–20 g of PMC3
- 1 syringe of PMC3 slip
- photocopy of design (figure A, figure B)
- 1 very soft black lead pencil
- 1 small roll of clear, plastic packing tape
- rubber printing-block material (such as Safety-Kut), at least 3" (7.5 cm) square
- 1 steel burnisher (jewelry burnisher, small steel knife handle, or the bowl of a steel spoon, for example)
- 1 linoleum carver or cutter with small V-shaped blade
- mild liquid dishwashing detergent
- 1 work surface (tempered glass or Plexiglas)
- 1 plastic roller
- 1 small bottle of olive oil (or other suitable lubricant)
- 1 piece of cellulose kitchen sponge, 1" (25 mm) square
- 1 porcelain or stainless-steel saucer or similar container (for the oiled sponge)
- 1 tissue blade
- 2 four-card stacks of playing cards
- 2 three-card stacks of playing cards
- 1 broader half of a plastic Easter egg (or 1 hard-boiled egg and drinking glass for support)
- 1 mug warmer
- 1 piece of copper mesh screen, 3" (7.5 cm) square
- 1 waterbrush (or small container of water and fine-tipped sable paintbrush)
- 1 color or clay shaper
- 1 art knife (X-Acto, for example)

The finished Enameled Dome Bead mirrors the colors of the coral, turquoise, and lapis lazuli, strung on hand-knotted silk.

"[Making art,] I felt that tiny click near the heart that meant: It was not bad.'" Lenore Tawney

- 1 steel drill bit, size #46–50 (with pin vise to hold drill bit, optional)
- salon boards, fine and coarse grit, or wet/dry emery paper, 220, 400, and 600 grit
- 1 PMC kiln
- 1 fireproof surface for the kiln with good, active ventilation
- 1 Kaowool insulated firing pad, 6" (15 cm) square
- 1 firing surface, kiln pad, or firebrick
- 1 pair long barbecue tongs
- 1 barbecue spatula
- 1 pair extra-heavy leather work gloves or potter's gloves (fire retardant)
- 1 large stainless-steel bowl filled with cool water
- 1 pair long steel tweezers
- 1 jeweler's brass brush
- 2 to 4 small paper cups or plastic yogurt containers
- 1 pair vinyl gloves
- 1 coarse fiberglass brush
- distilled water (if your tap water has a high mineral content)
- 1 bottle of Klyr-Fire (holding agent for enamels)
- 1 glass eyedropper
- 1 watercolor paint tray (with at least six depression or wells)
- good-quality dust mask or respirator
- 80-mesh enamels (see page 104)
- 1 penny or similarly sized small coin
- 1 a small enamel spatula or plastic spoon
- 1 small 100-mesh enamel sifter (with collector tray and cover, if possible)
- 2 small, clean glass jars
- 1 size 3/0 sable paintbrush (extra fine)
- 1 size 0 sable paintbrush
- 1 three-point firing trivet
- 1 trinket kiln (such as an UltraLite Kiln, with ceramic insert)
- 1 small spatula for the trinket kiln
- 1 pair light-filtering safety glasses designed for enameling or kiln work
- 1 timer or stopwatch
- 1 pair steel tweezers
- safety glasses for grinding work
- 1 rotary tool (such as flex shaft or Dremel)
- 1 heatless wheel (such as Mizzy)
- assorted 3M Scotch-Brite Radial Bristle Discs, in grits ranging from most coarse to micron fine
- 6–10 rotary-tool screw mandrels (for the heatless wheel and the radial bristle discs)
- 1 small bowl of water
- liver of sulfur (optional)
- magnetic tumbler (optional)
- polishing cloth (such as a Sunshine Cloth)

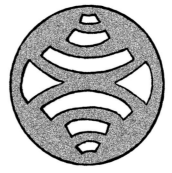

Figure A: Dome Pattern (actual size)   **Figure B: Backplate Pattern (actual size)**

MAKING THE BLOCKS

1. Photocopy the Dome Pattern and the Backplate Pattern drawings (figures A and B) at exact size.

2. Completely darken only the shaded areas of each of the patterns with the pencil (**A**).

A. Darken the shaded areas on each pattern.

B. Burnish the pattern onto the block, occasionally lifting a free edge of the pattern to check the transfer.

C. The pencil-shaded areas of the pattern have transferred to the surface of the block.

D. The carved areas of the block are the areas that will be raised in the metal clay after the block is pressed into it. Carve away from the hand holding the block.

3. Place the Dome Pattern, image side down, on the surface of the printing block, centering the pattern. Tape down one edge of the pattern with packing tape. Burnish the back of the image onto the block with the burnishing tool (**B, C**).

4. With the linoleum carver or cutter, carve out only the shaded areas of the block. Hold the carver in one hand and place the index finger of the other hand on the top of the carver, exerting a little downward pressure to control the forward movement of the tool. Carve the outer edge of the pattern first, then carve the rest of the pattern (**D**).

5. Repeat steps 3 and 4 to transfer the Backplate Pattern to the reverse side of the printing block.

6. Wash each carved surface with warm water and a little mild liquid dishwashing detergent. Dry with a soft, clean towel. Clean up your work area and remove all the carved particles.

MAKING THE DOME AND BACKPLATE

1. After taping the dull edge of the tissue blade for visibility, carefully and lightly lubricate the sharp edge and then your hands with the olive oil and the sponge. Lightly oil the work surface, the roller, the plastic egg half or the hardboiled egg, and the dome design side of the printing block.

2. Rest one four-card stack of playing cards along each edge on the work surface, leaving a space in between for rolling metal clay.

Safety Tip

When carving, work with great care. Keep your fingers clear of the cutting edge of the carver in case the tool slips from the block. Don't carve in the direction of the hand that is holding the block.

3. Roll a lump of PMC3 into a ball about 1" (2.5 cm) in diameter. With the palm of your hand, flatten the ball on the work surface. With the roller, roll the metal clay into a sheet, level with height of the cards, turning the metal clay several times to maintain an approximate circular shape. The finished sheet should be larger in diameter than the pattern on the printing block.

4. To make the dome, place the printing block on your worktable, with the dome design side up. Place a three-card stack on either side of the block. Add playing cards until the three-card stacks are raised completely above the surface of the block.

5. Working carefully with the tissue blade, lift the metal clay sheet off the work surface and lay it on the printing block, centering the sheet on the carved design.

6. With the roller, very firmly roll the metal clay onto the block, until the sheet is level with the three-card stack of cards. Lift a corner of the metal clay to check the image impression.

E. Trim the dome with the tissue blade while it is still on the armature.

7. Place the plastic egg (broad half only) on the work table, convex side up. (If you are using a hard-boiled egg as an armature, oil the larger end and rest it in the drinking glass, with the broad end up.) Carefully lift the metal clay sheet off the printing plate and drape it evenly over the egg, gently conforming it to the shape without distorting the impressed design.

8. With the tissue blade, carefully trim the bottom edge of the draped form so that it is at an even level **(E)**. Don't trim too much or too close to the indented sections of the design. Leave the dome on the form and set the form aside to air-dry.

9. Repeat steps 2–6, but this time oil and print with the block for the backplate design.

10. Trim the metal clay to form a circle that is a little larger than the diameter of the bottom edge of the dome. Set the backplate aside to dry on the copper screening on the mug warmer, flipping it frequently to avoid warping.

JOINING THE DOME, HOLE SUPPORTS, AND BACKPLATE

1. While the dome and backplate are drying, relubricate the tissue blade, roller, work surface, and your hands, if necessary. With the roller, roll out a sheet of metal clay on the work surface, level with a three-card stack of playing cards.

2. Working carefully with the tissue blade, cut out two very small triangles for the hole supports. They should be no larger than the spaces marked with an X on the "Placement of Hole Supports" drawing, figure C. Set the supports on the mug warmer to dry.

3. When the dome and the hole supports are completely dry, with the filled waterbrush or wet paintbrush, lightly moisten the two spots on the dome that correspond to the X's on the drawing.

4. Lightly moisten one side of each of the hole supports.

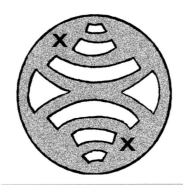

Figure C: Placement of Hole Supports (actual size)

F. Rotate the bit slowly to drill through the dome and hole support.

5. With the syringe, extrude a little slip onto the moistened area on one of the supports. Holding the dome with one finger inside it as support, press the hole support onto one of the moistened spots on the dome.

6. Repeat steps 4 and 5 to join the second hole support to the other X spot.

7. Set the dome aside on the mug warmer to dry.

8. With the waterbrush or wet paintbrush, make a dot of water at the center of each of the hole supports. Remove a little softened metal clay from that spot with the scribe to make a small depression in the metal clay.

9. Hold the dome with one finger inside it for support. Place the drill bit on the slight depression. Rotate the bit slowly to drill through to the inside of the inner wall. Don't push hard, or you'll hurt your finger when you break through. Simply let the drill bit gradually cut through the metal clay **(F)**.

ENAMELED DOME BEAD **103**

G. When the bead is suspended on the necklace, the small carved "ditch" will allow the chain or thread to move easily in the holes, without creating too much stress on it.

G. When the bead is suspended on the necklace, the small carved "ditch" will allow the chain or thread to move easily in the holes, without creating too much stress on it.

H. Work with a scribe to trace the shape of the dome onto the backplate.

Choosing Enamels

Enamels are sold as mixed-size grains and then are sifted to specific mesh sizes. The grids of the screens on enamel sifters come in a different number of openings per square inch (2.5 cm). The lower the number, the larger the spaces between the wires of the screen. The enamels for this project are sifted to 100 mesh, to yield large enamel grains that will produce clear transparent colors.

If you haven't worked with enamels before, I suggest that you choose cool colors (blues and greens). Reds, yellows, oranges, and pinks react with silver unless you take precautions—so it's easiest to start out with cool colors while you're still learning. For this project, choose transparent enamels. Be sure to select medium-expansion enamels designed for use with silver. I used lead-free Thompson Transparent Enamels: Sky Blue, Sea, and Spring.

For this project, you'll be applying five layers of enamel. You can fire each layer, except for the final layer, to what looks like a bumpy orange peel. The final layer will be fired to a glassy, smooth surface. Every kiln has its own idiosyncrasies, however, so remember to check the bead while it's firing—and don't forget to wear the safety glasses!

10. Turn over the dome and lightly moisten a spot near each hole. With the art knife, remove a small amount of softened metal clay to make a very small "ditch" (**G**).

11. If the edges of the holes aren't smooth, moisten the opening. Rotate the shaper in the holes to smooth the edges.

12. Place the backplate on the work surface, smooth side up.

13. Place the dome on the backplate and scribe a very light mark into the backplate, tracing the perimeter of the dome (**H**).

14. With the syringe, extrude slip on the scribed line and slightly within it. Apply more slip than you think you might need—you can clean up and recycle the extra slip later. Any excess slip inside the joint will not be visible but will strengthen the joint (**I**).

15. Align the patterns on the dome and backplate so that, even though they are slightly different, the lines of the patterns will be approximately parallel. Gently press the dome onto the slip line on the backplate to join them. Hold the dome with the fingers of one hand and the backplate with the fingers of the other hand to avoid putting too much pressure on either. Rotate the dome back and forth a little to make a secure joint, then realign.

16. Allow the dome bead to dry on the mug warmer. Then check for gaps or cracks and repair them with slip. Dry the bead again. Clean up the excess dried slip on the outside.

17. Sand the joint smooth with salon boards or emery paper. With the art knife, pop off any excess dried slip around the edges and hole supports. Refine the edges with finer and finer Tri-M-Ite papers. Remember, in this greenware (unfired) state, the metal clay is somewhat fragile. If the holes are blocked with slip, clear them by adding a little water and rotating the drill bit very gently in each hole. (Dry the bit thoroughly afterward to prevent rusting.)

I. Don't worry about applying too much slip to the scribed line. The excess that seeps inside helps strengthen the joint.

FIRING THE BEAD

1. Place the Kaowool firing pad on the firing surface, kiln pad, or firebrick in a cold PMC kiln.

2. Place the bead, backplate side down, on the firing pad and close the kiln door.

3. Turn on the kiln and select the program that will allow the kiln to run for 2 hours at 1650°F (900°C). Follow the manufacturer's instructions for programming your kiln.

4. After the kiln has completed the firing cycle, allow it to cool down a little. Then open the door to allow it to cool down even more.

5. Check the digital readout of the temperature on the kiln and, after the kiln has cooled down, put on the heavy gloves and move the bead with tweezers either to another fireproof surface to air-cool or into a large stainless-steel bowl filled with cool water to quench it.

ADDING THE LAYERS OF ENAMEL

1. Review the sidebar Choosing Enamels on the facing page.

2. Working with a jeweler's brass brush and the liquid dishwashing detergent, remove the white, matte silver oxides from the surface of the bead.

3. If you have a magnetic tumbler, tumble the bead for about 15 minutes. Then sand the bead with 600-grit emery paper to refine surface flaws. (Depending on how bright a finish you want, you can continue to sand with microfinishing papers.) Brass-brush the bead with liquid dishwashing detergent and warm water. If you don't have a magnetic tumbler, there are number of alternate ways to finish the surface of the bead (see pages 25–27).

4. Before applying enamels, the bead must be dry and clean. Put on the vinyl gloves and wash the bead, scrubbing the surface with a coarse fiberglass brush under running water. Brush all over the bead, making certain to brush in the indented areas.

Tip

Wearing vinyl gloves while washing the bead protects your fingers from getting any fiberglass splinters from the brush.

5. Fill one of the paper cups half full of water. (If your tap water has a high mineral content, use distilled water.) Fill another cup half full of Klyr-Fire. A fifty-fifty mixture will help hold the enamels in place on your bead before the bead is fired.

6. Squeeze the eye dropper in the water to fill it. Squeeze out the water into one of the wells in the watercolor paint tray. Squeeze the dropper again to fill it with Klyr-Fire and squeeze to deposit the Klyr-Fire in the same well as the water. The solution will be approximately one-half water and one-half Klyr-Fire. Set the tray aside with a piece of clean paper towel over it.

7. Put on the dust mask or respirator.

Working with Enamels

Enamels are very finely ground glass. It is unsafe to work with dry enamels, even lead-free enamels, without wearing a good dust mask. When you remove the mask, place it in a large, clean plastic bag so that it doesn't get contaminated with glass or other types of dust. When you are finished working, store the enamels in their original package or in another clean container, away from direct light. Thoroughly wet-mop the surface of your work area to completely remove any stray enamel powders. Wash your hands and hair thoroughly.

J. Moisten the enamel in the tray well with a single drop of the fifty-fifty mixture of Klyr-Fire and water, allowing the enamel grains to absorb the water.

K. Paint enamel into the depressions of the dome and backplate with the size 3/0 sable paintbrush.

8. Place a piece of clean white paper on your worktable and place the sifter on top. Use the spoon to transfer a small amount of one of your blue enamels, about ½ teaspoon at the most, to the 100-mesh sifter. Place the coin in the sifter. Hold a clean paper cup over the top of the sifter to avoid excess glass dust from escaping. Shake the sifter, causing the coin to push the finest grains of enamel through the mesh. (If you have a lid and collector tray for the sifter, substitute those for the paper and the cup.)

9. After the dust has settled in the sifter, lift off the paper cup or lid and remove the sifter from the paper or collector tray. You'll work with the large, coarse grains that remain in the sifter. Transfer the finer grains from the paper or tray into a small glass jar and set aside for future use. You'll need no more than about ½ teaspoon of each sifted enamel color.

10. Transfer the large grains to one of the empty wells in the watercolor paint tray.

11. Fill the dropper with the fifty-fifty Klyr-Fire solution. Hold the dropper along the edge of the well with the enamel grains. Deposit one drop of the solution along the sloping side of the well, allowing it to be absorbed by the enamel. Don't flood the enamel—add more solution only to barely moisten the enamel, if needed. Do not stir or mix (**J**).

12. Hold the bead in one hand. With the size 0 sable paintbrush, apply a little of the Klyr-Fire solution to one of the depressions of the design on the dome side of the bead. Set that brush aside.

Use the size 3/0 sable paintbrush to lift some wet enamel and place it in a small area at one end of that depression. Continue this process until you've put some of the same color in all of the depressions on the dome side of the bead (**K**).

13. Turn over the bead and repeat step 12 to apply enamel in the depressions on the backplate. The fifty-fifty mixture will hold the enamel on the dome in place. If your brush becomes overladen with enamel grains, simply wash it off in a cup of plain water. It may look like the depressions in the bead are already filled, but this is just the first layer of enamel grains for the first firing. This project bead has five layers of enamel (five firings).

14. Set the bead on the trivet on your worktable to air-dry completely. Or set the trivet on the mug warmer or on top of the hot kiln (**L**). When dry, the enamels will look somewhat powdery. They must be completely dry before firing. If not, the grains will pop off in the kiln or the enamel will "crawl" on the surface of the bead later, leaving some areas bare.

L. Dry the enamels by placing the bead on a trivet and then on a hot kiln. (The photo shows the UltraLite kiln with the ceramic insert under the trivet on the lid of the kiln.)

15. If you are working with a trinket kiln, place the kiln on a fireproof surface near active ventilation. This small kiln is useful for firing small pieces and is more economical to fire than a larger kiln, although you can fire enamels in a standard PMC kiln. (If you are working with an UltraLite Kiln, as I did, place the ceramic insert accessory on the kiln lid during the firing to maintain the temperature required to fuse the enamels. When you've finished firing, move the insert to a fireproof surface before lifting the lid of the kiln.)

16. Turn on the ventilation fan. Plug in the trinket kiln and bring it up to temperature, following the manufacturer's instructions. Or turn on the PMC kiln and select the program.

17. Wash and completely dry your sifting tools and brushes. Discard the fifty-fifty mixture if there are grains of enamel in it and make another batch.

18. Repeat steps 7–17 with a second enamel color and then with the third enamel color. Keep a written record of the colors you have used for each firing and where on the bead you've placed them. It helps to do a rough drawing of the bead and add your notes there.

FIRING THE ENAMELS

1. Plug in the trinket kiln (if you are working with the UltraLite kiln, place the ceramic insert on the top now). It takes about 15 minutes to ½ hour or more for a trinket kiln to come to temperature. The temperature for firing enamels is around 1500° F (815° C). You can use a digital pyrometer to determine when the kiln has reached the proper temperature—but it's easy to tell without one because the coils will glow a bright orange red when the kiln is hot enough (be sure to wear safety glasses when you view the coils).

2. When the kiln is at temperature, put on the heavy gloves. Working with the small spatula and the long tweezers, transfer the trivet, with the bead still on it, onto the kiln heating surface. Place the kiln lid on the kiln. If you are working with a trinket kiln, place the ceramic insert on top of the kiln lid to help keep the heat constant.

3. Allow the kiln to come back up to temperature and set the timer for 2–3 minutes.

4. Wearing safety glasses, lift the lid for a quick peek at about the 2-minute mark to see if the enamels have fused. For each firing, except for the last, fire the enamels until the surface looks like a bumpy orange peel. The final layer should be fired to a glassy, smooth surface. Every kiln has its own idiosyncrasies, so remember to check the bead frequently while it's firing (and don't forget to wear the safety glasses!).

5. When the enamels have fused, put on the heavy gloves and use the spatula to move the trivet to a fireproof surface.

6. Remove the bead from the trivet with a pair of clean tweezers and move it to a fireproof surface. Do not quench the bead. Quenching will cause thermal shock, which will crack the enamels. Allow the bead to come to room temperature, about 5–10 minutes. Be careful. The bead and the trivet may look cool, but looks can be deceiving. Allow a sufficient amount of time for them to cool before touching the bead with your hand. You can tell if the bead has cooled if you feel no heat when you hold your hand abour 4" (10 cm) above it. Unplug the kiln.

7. Put on the vinyl gloves and scrub the bead with the fiberglass brush under warm running water. Then rinse the bead, holding it by its edges. Washing will remove any invisible oxides that formed during the firing and will prepare the surface for a new layer of fresh enamel granules.

8. Repeat the entire process, beginning with step 7 of Adding the Layers of Enamel through the washing step above, for each of the colors for the second, third, and fourth layers of enamels. If you run out of the larger grains of a color, sift more (cover the paint tray when you sift and try not to sift near it.)

9. Now repeat the steps again to apply a fifth layer of enamel, but do not fire this layer as you did the others. Instead, fire to a smooth, glassy surface. Monitor the firing, wearing safety glasses, as this firing may take a little longer time than the earlier firings. You don't have to scrub with the fiberglass brush after this final firing.

For a Glassy Enamel Surface

The Enameled Dome Bead project instructions produce a bead with enamels that have a matte, translucent finish. If you want to the enamels to have a glassy, smooth surface, scrub once again with the fiberglass brush, after grinding and polishing the metal. Reheat the trinket kiln. Place the bead on the trivet, return it to the pre-heated kiln, and fuse the enamels once again, as explained in Firing the Enamels (see page 107). Allow the bead to cool and continue with step 7 of the instructions for firing.

Tip

To mount the radial bristle discs on their mandrels, check out the direction in which the rotary tool rotates and mount the discs so that the bristles will rotate smoothly across the metal in that direction.

FINISHING THE BEAD

1. Put on the dust mask and the safety glasses for grinding. (They may feel cumbersome, but your eyes and lungs will thank you.)

2. Insert the heatless wheel mandrel in the rotary tool. Please follow all manufacturer's instructions for working with these tools safely. (If you're working with the flex-shaft machine, make sure that it's grounded.)

3. Grind the metal and enamel surface of the bead until it is level and the enamel has a matte finish.

4. Dip the bead into the bowl of water and grind a little more, until the surface of the enamel is no longer glassy. Keep the bead wet while grinding the enamels, but dry it frequently to determine when the enamel surface is smooth and matte.

5. Make sure there aren't any stray granules of fused enamels on the metal surface of your bead. If there are, remove them with the Mizzy heatless wheel. Use the radial bristle discs mounted on screw mandrels to remove the lines on the metal that the Mizzy wheel makes, starting with the coarsest disc and proceeding through the range of grits. Continue until there are no more scratches and the metal is smooth and shiny. Keep the bristle discs out of contact with the enamels.

Tip

Tumbling the fired bead in a magnetic or other rotary-style tumbler will bring up a bright finish and should not damage the enamels. Run a pipe cleaner through the holes in the bead to keep the tumbling shot from collecting inside the bead. After tumbling and rinsing the bead, rub it with the polishing cloth to bring up the shine on the metal.

You can achieve brighter finishes with further machine or hand polishing. If you want the enamels to have a glassy, rather than a matte, finish, see the sidebar above left—but if you like what you've achieved so far, continue to step 6.

6. If desired, patinate the bead with liver of sulfur (see page 148). If you don't want to patinate, continue to step 7.

7. Rub the bead vigorously with a polishing cloth. Then wash the bead in warm soapy water.

River Summer Bead

ARTIST: Linda Kaye-Moses
MATERIAL: fine silver, sterling silver, vitreous enamel, lapis lazuli, Tibetan turquoise, silk
TECHNIQUES: metal clay, carved-plate printing, enameling, patination
DIMENSIONS: 1³/₁₆" high × 1¾" wide × 1" deep (3 cm × 4.5 cm × 2.5 cm)

SKILL LEVEL: Advanced
FINISHED SIZE: 1½" high × 1" wide × ½" deep
(35 mm × 25 mm × 13 mm)

Double-Sided BEAD

"An acrylic gel medium makes a versatile printing plate."

In this project,

you'll make a double-sided, hollow bead. The printing plate for the metal clay surface design is made with an acrylic gel medium. I used a sand-texture acrylic medium for the frontplate and backplate, but you can choose other mediums available at art or craft supply stores.

The complex bead structure consists of six parts: three graduated rectangular layers (the frontplate/backplate first layer, second layer, and third layer) stacked on top of each other and duplicated on each side of the bead. These joined layers are supported and separated by a cylindrical inner ring. You will texture each of the layers and the inner ring individually.

The finished Double-Sided Bead is the centerpiece of this strand of serpentine, strung on hand-knotted silk.

"What I've done exposes a little bit of a part of me, that isn't me, to myself." Dogon sculptor

What You Will Need

- about 33 g of PMC3
- 1 jar of gel medium (such as sand-texture)
- 1 container of PMC3 slip
- assorted containers (paper cups or yogurt containers, for example)
- 1 palette knife
- 1 flat, soft oil or watercolor paintbrush
- assorted pieces of corrugated cardboard or paper of similar weight, about 2" × 4" (5 × 10 cm)
- color or clay shapers
- texturing tools (combs, scribes, or sewing needles, for example)
- 1 mug warmer
- 1 hair dryer (optional)
- 1 small bottle of olive oil (or other suitable lubricant)
- 1 piece of cellulose kitchen sponge, 1" (25 mm) square
- 1 porcelain or stainless-steel saucer or similar container (for the oiled sponge)
- 1 work surface (tempered glass or Plexiglas)
- 1 tissue blade
- 1 plastic roller
- 2 four-card stacks of playing cards
- 2 three-card stacks of playing cards
- 1 piece of copper mesh screen, 3" (7.5 cm) square
- 1 pair fine-tip, small tweezers
- assorted playing cards
- 2 rubber stamps with shallow allover patterns
- 2 jeweler's or leather-design stamping punches or letterpress ornaments, with different designs
- 1 wooden dowel, about ¾" (19 mm) in diameter
- assorted salon boards or wet/dry emery paper in several grits
- 1 ruler
- 1 waterbrush (or small container of water and fine-tipped sable paintbrush)

B. Experiment by "drawing" with acrylic gel medium on a piece of cardboard to choose the texture you'd like for your bead. Make as many experimental plates as you'd like.

- 1 scribe
- 1 syringe of PMC3 slip
- 1 art knife (X-Acto, for example)
- 1 steel drill bit, size #46–50 (with pin vise to hold drill bit, optional)
- 1 PMC kiln
- 1 fireproof surface for the kiln with good, active ventilation
- 1 small cup or scoop
- 1 small fireproof container (a terra-cotta flowerpot saucer or shallow stainless-steel bowl, for example)
- alumina hydrate (enough to fill small fireproof container)
- 1 firing surface, kiln pad, or firebrick
- 1 pair long barbecue tongs
- 1 barbecue spatula
- 1 pair extra-heavy leather work gloves or potter's gloves (fire retardant)
- 1 large stainless-steel bowl filled with cool water
- 1 pair long steel tweezers

MAKING THE PRINTING PLATES

1. With the palette knife, scoop a small amount of the acrylic medium into a small container. Close the original container to keep the medium from drying out or becoming contaminated by dust.

2. Thinly spread a layer of acrylic medium (three to four playing cards thick) onto a piece of cardboard with the palette knife or paintbrush **(A)**.

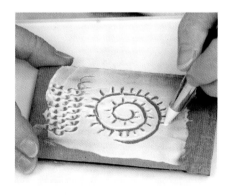

A. Draw texture with a color shaper in gel medium to make the printing plate.

3. Add texture to the medium by drawing in it with a shaper, a comb, scribes, or other tools. Lift the tool occasionally and wipe it clean with a paper towel before proceeding. If you don't like your pattern, wipe the surface clean with a paper towel or begin again with a fresh piece of cardboard. Experiment by making several different patterns in the acrylic medium **(B)**.

4. Allow the acrylic on the cardboard to dry overnight. You could also dry it more quickly with the hair dryer or with the mug warmer (but don't leave it unattended). Don't try to use the cardboard for printing if the acrylic is even slightly tacky.

5. Lightly oil the printing plate and press a little bit of metal clay onto it to preview the texture. If you like the results, proceed. If not, repeat the process to make a new plate.

MAKING THE FRONTPLATE AND BACKPLATE

1. After taping the dull edge of the tissue blade for visibility, carefully and lightly lubricate the sharp edge and then your hands and the olive oil and the sponge. Select one of your printing plate "experiments." Lubricate your hands, one printing plate, the work surface, and roller.

2. Roll a lump of PMC3 into a ball, about ½" (12 mm) in diameter, between your hands. Place the metal clay lump on the work surface and flatten it slightly.

3. Place a four-card stack of playing cards on either side of the flattened lump. With the roller, roll the lump into a sheet, level with height of the cards.

4. Working carefully with the tissue blade, lift the metal clay sheet off the work surface and place it on the oiled printing plate.

Tip

To adjust for the thickness of the printing plate, raise the level of the card stacks by placing pieces of corrugated cardboard or extra playing cards under each one to achieve the correct level.

C. Dry the metal clay rectangles on the mug warmer.

5. Place a three-card stack of playing cards on either side of the metal clay sheet and, using the roller, roll the sheet onto the printing plate, level with height of the cards.

6. With the tissue blade, trim the textured metal clay sheet to a rectangle that measures 1⅞" × 1¼" (5 cm × 3 cm).

7. Place the metal clay rectangle on the mug warmer to dry (**C**). If the metal clay seems to be warping, place the copper screening beneath it. It will also help to turn the metal clay rectangle several times while it is drying to limit the warping, too.

8. Repeat steps 2–7, matching the dimensions of the first rectangle. The two rectangles form the frontplate and backplate, the first layer of the bead.

MAKING THE SECOND LAYERS

1. Oil both rubber stamps. You'll use them to print each of the second layers—one to add to the frontplate and one for the backplate, so the bead will have different designs on each side. (If you prefer, you could print the same design on both sides of the bead.

2. Roll a lump of PMC3 into a ball, about ½" (12 mm) in diameter, between your hands (re-oil your hands if needed). Place the metal clay lump on the work surface and flatten it slightly.

3. Place a three-card stack of playing cards on either side of the metal clay. Working with the roller, roll the lump into a sheet, level with height of cards.

4. Place the rubber stamp on top of the metal clay sheet, design side down, and gently but firmly roll the pattern onto the metal clay.

5. Working carefully with the tissue blade, cut out two rectangles that measure 1¼" × ¾" (3 cm × 2 cm). Set them aside to dry on the copper screening on the mug warmer.

MAKING THE THIRD LAYERS

1. Lightly oil the stamping punches or letterpress ornaments and the work surface. Relubricate the roller, tissue blade, and your hands, too, if needed.

2. Roll a small lump of PMC3 between your hands to form a ball approximately ½" (12 mm) in diameter. Place the metal clay lump on the work surface and flatten it slightly.

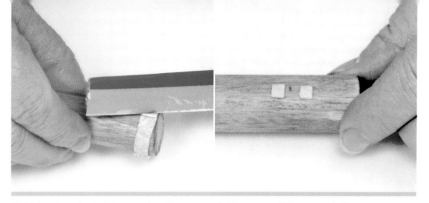

D. Make a bevel cut at the overlapping ends of the inner ring.

E. The curve of the square hole supports should conform to the curve of the inner ring, so both hole supports are dried on the dowel.

3. Place a three-card stack of playing cards on either side of the metal clay. With the roller, roll the lump into a sheet, level with height of the cards.

4. Gently press one of the punches or letterpress ornaments into the metal clay sheet. Move the tool at least 1" (2.5 cm) away from the impression and press again with the other punch or ornament. (Or use the same design tool to make an impression on both of the third layers.)

5. Working carefully with the tissue blade, cut a small rectangle around each impression, about ¾" × ⅜" (2 cm × 1 cm).

6. Place the rectangles on the mug warmer to dry completely.

MAKING THE INNER RING

1. After taping the dull edge of the tissue blade for visibility, carefully and lightly lubricate the sharp edge and then your hands with the olive oil and the sponge. Lightly oil the roller, printing plate, work surface, and dowel.

2. Roll a lump of PMC3 into a long cigar shape with your hands. Place the metal clay lump on the work surface and flatten it slightly.

3. Place a five-card stack of playing cards on each side of the metal clay. With the roller, roll the lump into a sheet, level with height of the cards.

4. Place a four-card stack of playing cards on each side of the printing plate and place the metal clay sheet on the plate. Roll the metal clay sheet to the level of the four-card stack. (Adjust the height as needed by adding corrugated cardboard or extra playing cards under the card stacks.)

5. Trim the textured PMC sheet to a strip about 1¼" wide (3.2 cm) and no more than 2⅝" (6.7 cm) long.

6. Wrap the strip around the dowel, allowing the ends to overlap, forming a perfect cylinder. Partially dry (15–30 seconds) on the mug warmer.

7. Working carefully with the tissue blade, trim the overlapped ends at an oblique angle, or bevel **(D)**. Beveling the ends enlarges the area that will be joined with slip, making for a stronger joint. Join the ends with water and slip.

8. Rest the dowel seam side down on the mug warmer. Let dry slightly (about 1–3 minutes). Slide the inner ring off the dowel and add slip to the inside of the seam.

9. Set the inner ring on the mug warmer to dry completely. Check it every so often for warping and adjust the shape as needed with your fingers. The ring will be hot, so remember to lift it off the mug warmer with tweezers and wait until it's cool before adjusting the shape.

MAKING THE HOLE SUPPORTS

1. If necessary, relubricate the work surface, tissue blade, roller, and your hands.

2. Roll a lump of PMC3 between your hands to form a ball about ¼" (6 mm) in diameter. Place the metal clay lump on the work surface and flatten it slightly.

3. Place the three-card stack of playing cards on each side of the flattened lump. With the roller, roll the lump into a sheet, level with height of the cards.

4. Working carefully with the tissue blade, cut out two squares that are slightly less than ¼" (6 mm) long on each side.

5. To create a curve to match the curve of the inner wall, lift one of the square hole supports and rest it on the dowel. The two edges of the square should be parallel to the length of the dowel. Repeat to shape the second hole support **(E)**.

6. Place the dowel on the mug warmer and dry the holes supports completely.

JOINING THE INNER RING AND HOLE SUPPORTS

1. When the hole supports and inner ring are completely dry, moisten a spot on the outer surface of the inner ring with the filled waterbrush or wet paintbrush. Also lightly moisten a spot on the concave surface (inside curve) of one of the hole supports.

2. Add PMC3 slip to the moistened spot on the inner ring. Gently press the moistened surface of the hole support onto that spot. To prevent the cylinder from cracking, keep one finger inside the inner ring, under the hole support, as you press. Or insert a small wooden dowel into the inner ring instead.

3. Repeat step 2 to join the second hole support to the opposite side of the inner ring (**F**).

4. With the small shaper, remove excess slip and smooth the joints. Dry completely.

DRILLING THE HOLES

1. Sand the edges of the inner ring completely flat and even with salon boards or emery papers. Measure the height of the inner ring with the ruler to make sure the height is consistent all the way around the form.

2. With the filled waterbrush or wet paintbrush, add a drop of water in the center of each of the hole supports. Then scrape those spots slightly with the scribe.

3. Place one finger inside the inner ring, under one of the moistened spots, to support the ring as you drill. Place the drill bit on the moistened spot and rotate it slowly, hand-drilling through to the inside of the ring. Do not push hard. Let the drill bit do the work (**G**).

4. If the edges of the holes aren't smooth, moisten the opening and rotate the shaper in the holes to smooth the edges.

JOINING THE PARTS

1. When all sections of the bead are completely dry, refine and sand the edges with salon boards or emery papers. Repair any cracks with slip.

2. With the filled waterbrush or wet paintbrush, lightly moisten the center of the textured side of the frontplate. Also moisten the untextured side of one of the second layers.

3. With the syringe, apply slip to the moistened side of the second layer with the shaper. Press the second layer onto the moistened area of the frontplate. Smooth the joint with the shaper, removing any excess slip. Set aside to dry on the mug warmer.

4. Repeat steps 2 and 3 to join the remaining second layer to the backplate.

5. Lightly moisten the center of the second layer (on the frontplate) and the untextured side of one of the third layers.

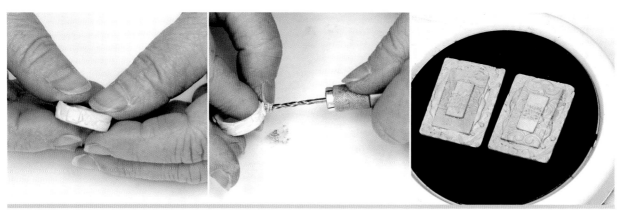

F. Join hole supports to opposite sides of the inner ring.

G. As the drill bit approaches the inside of the inner ring, it may catch a little. Simply back it out of the hole, turn it a little, reinsert it in the hole, and begin to rotate it again.

H. Join the second and third layers to the frontplate and backplate.

I. Scribe a line around the inner ring, on the smooth side of the frontplate assembly.

J. The hole supports on the inner ring should face a long side of the frontplate.

K. The backplate and frontplate edges should align in the assembled bead.

6. With the syringe, extrude slip onto the moistened side of the third layer. Press that spot onto the moistened area on the second layer. Smooth the joint with the shaper, removing any excess slip. Set aside to dry.

7. Repeat steps 5 and 6 to join the second layer (on the backplate) to the remaining third layer (**H**).

8. When all sections are dry, place the inner ring onto the smooth (untextured) side of the frontplate assembly, slightly above center. Draw a very light line all around the inner ring with the scribe (**I**).

9. Moisten one edge of the inner ring and the scribed line on the frontplate.

10. With the syringe, extrude a line of slip along the scribed line. To apply a nice thick line of slip, don't put the tip on the syringe.

11. Press the inner ring onto the line of slip, so that each hole support on the inner ring faces a long side of the rectangular frontplate (**J**). Rotate the pieces a little to secure the joint. Then realign them.

12. Let the slip ooze out of the joint and then smooth it immediately with a shaper. Add more slip to the inside of the inner ring joint. (You don't need to smooth this slip; it won't be visible.) Set the joined assembly on the mug warmer to dry completely.

13. Repeat steps 9–12 to attach the backplate to the inner ring. Make sure that the backplate and frontplate edges are aligned (**K**). Set the bead aside to dry on the mug warmer.

14. When the bead is completely dry, smooth rough spots with water and the shaper. Blend in any excess slip.

FIRING THE BEAD

1. Put on the respirator or dust mask and vinyl gloves. Fill the small fireproof container with alumina hydrate.

2. Place the bead on top of the alumina hydrate. Then place the container on the firing surface, kiln pad, or firebrick in a cold kiln. Close the kiln door.

3. Turn on the active ventilation, then turn on the kiln. Select the program that will allow the kiln to run for 2 hours at 1650°F (900°C).

4. After the kiln has completed the firing cycle, allow it to cool down a little. Then open the door to allow it to cool down even more.

5. Check the digital readout of the temperature on the kiln and, after the kiln has cooled down, put on the heavy gloves and move the bead with tweezers either to another fireproof surface to air-cool or into a large stainless-steel bowl filled with cool water to quench it.

6. Finish and polish bead (see page 25).

Vessel BEAD

SKILL LEVEL: Advanced
FINISHED SIZE: 1½" high × by 1⅜" wide × ½" deep
(38 mm × 35 mm × 13 mm)

"This Vessel Bead is embellished with spirals and set with a gemstone."

What You Will Need

- 23–24 g of PMC3
- 1 container of PMC3 slip
- 1 smooth stone in oval or other shape (Choose a fairly even and symmetrical stone, or choose papier-mâché or polymer clay.)
- 1 permanent fine marker
- 1 work surface (tempered glass or Plexiglas)
- 1 small bottle of olive oil (or other suitable lubricant)
- 1 piece of cellulose kitchen sponge, 1" (25 mm) square
- 1 porcelain or stainless-steel saucer or similar container (for the oiled sponge)
- 1 tissue blade
- 1 plastic roller
- 2 four-card stacks of playing cards
- 1 rubber stamp, not too deep a pattern (that will fit the dimensions of the stone armature)

- 2 three-card stacks of playing cards
- extra playing cards
- 1 pair scissors
- 1 brass clay cutter or short length of brass tubing, about 1¼" (32 mm) in diameter
- 1 mug warmer
- 1 paper lollipop stick
- color or clay shapers
- assorted salon boards in several grits
- wet/dry emery paper in several grits
- 1 small, dry, flat paintbrush
- 2 five-card stacks of playing cards
- brass circle cutters or short lengths of brass tubing in various diameters (from ⅛" [3 mm], depending on the dimensions of the finished neck lip)

This Vessel Bead

is shaped like a small vase with spirals. The body is made the same way as the body of the Belted Dome Bead (see page 92). A smooth oval stone serves as the armature, or you can instead make the armature from cork clay, wood clay, or papier-mâché (see page 94).

Making and attaching the spirals requires a delicate touch and could be classified as an advanced-plus technique. You can add the spirals or skip them entirely.

The project also includes instructions for embedding a premade, fine silver bezel cup in fresh metal clay. The premade cup has small tabs protruding from the bottom. When the cup is fired, the metal clay shrinks around the tabs, forming a strong mechanical lock with the bezel. The gemstone is set after every other step has been completed.

The finished Vessel Bead, strung as a pendant with hand-knotted silk on a necklace of garnet beads.

"If there was no Art, there would be nothing on Earth."
Tewa Pueblo child

Choosing the Model

Your smooth stone will be the model for forming the two sides of your bead. If you're working with a natural form, the shape won't be completely symmetrical—that's why you mark each side. When you drape your metal clay on the stone, you'll know which side is which—helpful when it comes time to fit the two sides together. You can find a smooth stone in nature, or in gardening supply stores.

You could also make your model from papier-mâché or polymer clay (follow the manufacturer's instructions). Sand the form with wet/dry emery paper. Then wet-mop the worktable and remove any residue. Wash your hands afterward to prevent the transfer of dust to your metal clay. To make the model from papier-mâché, see the sidebar on page 94.

- 1 waterbrush (or small container of water and fine-tipped sable paintbrush)
- 1 art knife (X-Acto, for example)
- 1 Makin's Ultimate Clay Extruder or other small extruder (If you do not have an extruder, see page 122.)
- 1 extruder die with a single narrow rectangular hole
- 1 piece of copper mesh screen, about 3" (7.5 cm) square
- 1 steel drill bit, size #46–50 (with pin vise to hold drill bit, optional)
- 1 steel drill bit larger than the one above
- 1 4 mm premade, fine silver bezel cup (Metal Clay Findings only, see page 150)
- 1 4 mm gemstone, low dome, calibrated to fit a 4 mm bezel cup (Measure stone and test in bezel cup before buying)
- 1 PMC kiln
- 1 fireproof surface for the kiln with active ventilation

- alumina hydrate (enough to fill small fireproof container)
- 1 small cup or scoop
- 1 small fireproof container (a terra-cotta flowerpot saucer or shallow stainless-steel bowl, for example)
- 1 respirator or good-quality dust mask
- 1 pair vinyl gloves
- 1 firing surface, kiln pad, or firebrick
- 1 pair long barbecue tongs
- 1 barbecue spatula
- 1 pair extra-heavy leather work gloves or potter's gloves (fire retardant)
- 1 large stainless-steel bowl filled with cool water
- 1 pair long steel tweezers
- assorted polishing and finishing tools and supplies
- 1 container of dental floss
- 1 large pinch Sticky wax (optional)
- 1 bezel pusher
- 1 polishing cloth (such as a Sunshine cloth)

MARKING THE STONE MODEL

1. Mark one surface of the model as #1 and the other as #2.

2. Mark two small lines at the center of one of the long sides of the model. These lines indicate where the neck of the vessel will be.

3. Draw a line around the "equator" (curve) of the stone **(A)**. The stone will act as a support on which to build two separate domes and will not be fired.

A. Mark one surface of the model with the numeral 1. Mark two lines at the center of a long side and one around the equator.

B. Trim the textured sheet of metal clay so the ends hang a little more than halfway down the sides of the stone.

C. Punch a semicircle with an oiled circle cutter.

MAKING THE BODY OF THE VESSEL

1. After taping the dull edge of the tissue blade for visibility, carefully and lightly lubricate the sharp edge and then your hands with the olive oil and the sponge. Lightly oil the rubber stamp, work surface, roller, and the model.

2. Place a lump of PMC3, about ¾" (19 mm) in diameter, on the work surface and flatten it slightly.

3. Place one four-card stack of playing cards on each side of the flattened lump and, working with the roller, roll the lump into a sheet, level with the cards. The perimeter of the sheet should be larger than the perimeter of the stone at the equator.

4. Use the tissue blade to lift the metal clay sheet off the work surface and lay it on the rubber stamp.

5. Place one three-card stack of playing cards on each side of the rubber stamp. Add playing cards underneath each three-card stack until the stack is raised completely above the surface of the rubber stamp.

6. With the roller, very firmly roll the metal clay onto the rubber stamp, almost level with height of the three-card stacks. (Lift a corner of the metal clay to see if the image transferred well from the rubber stamp. If not, replace the corner and roll again.) You may need to remove playing cards to adjust the height of the stack.

7. Remove the PMC3 sheet from the rubber stamp and drape it on the #1 side of the stone. Don't stretch it to fit. If it's not large enough, roll it out again (steps 2–6).

8. With the scissors, trim the draped PMC3 sheet so that the sides hang a little more than halfway down the sides of the stone, but don't stretch it around the equator of the stone **(B)**. If it extends too much past the equator, it may be difficult to remove the metal clay sheet without breaking it. Trim only the excess material. Leave enough material so that when you trim and sand it in later steps, you still retain enough of a curve. Follow the equator line as guide.

9. Oil the ¼-inch (6 mm) circle cutter and use it to punch out a semicircle (smaller is better) from the long side of the dome, where you marked the two lines on the model (where the neck of the vessel will be attached) **(C)**.

10. Set the stone with the draped PMC3 onto a mug warmer, bare stone side down. Dry it to leather hard (it should feel dry, but still be a little pliable). Again cut away any material that overhangs the equator of the stone. The PMC3 sheet should now retain the domed shape of half of the stone, and you can remove it from the stone and trim it further, if needed. This is the first of the two dome shapes you will need to make your bead. Dry it completely.

11. Repeat steps 2–10 to make the second dome of the vessel body, but this time, form it on the #2 side of the model.

MAKING THE NECK

1. While the domes are drying, make the neck. It's a simple tube form with a flat lip at the top. Again lubricate the roller, a tissue blade, your hands, and the work surface.

2. Place a lump of PMC3, about 1" (25 mm) in diameter, on the work surface and flatten it slightly.

3. Place one three-card stack of playing cards on each side of the flattened lump and, using the roller, roll the lump into a sheet level with height of the cards.

4. Trim the metal clay sheet to a rectangle about 5/8" × 3/4" (16 mm × 19 mm).

5. Roll the 5/8" (16 mm) sides to thin them a little. The thinned ends create more surface area for a stronger joint.

D. Form the neck around a paper stick.

6. Wrap the PMC3 rectangle around a short length of paper lollipop stick, overlapping the thinned ends. By overlapping the ends, you will be able to maintain the same thickness around the entire tube. Leave at least 7/8" (23 mm) of the stick protruding at one end and a 1/8" (3 mm) extension of metal clay "tube" at the other end.

7. Use the tissue blade to cut through the overlapping ends at an angle, to bevel the ends.

8. With a shaper, apply PMC3 slip to one of the ends and join the ends to form a seam. Use the shaper to confirm the joint. Try to make it snug, but don't stretch it. The tube may already be a little loose on the stick. Add extra slip to the outside of the seam **(D)**.

9. Set the neck aside to dry. Then, sand and refine the surfaces, seams, and edges, removing excess slip. Remove the paper stick, if it's loose. If it's stuck, rotate the stick gently to remove it or, if necessary, trim it to the edge of the neck with a side cutter and sand it down, right to the edge. You can fire the remnant of the stick with the bead. (Don't add any of the sanding dust to your container of dust for slip; instead, add it to a container of dust to send to a refiner for recycling.)

MAKING THE NECK LIP

1. The neck lip is shaped like a thick flattened doughnut. Place a lump of PMC3, about 1/2" (13 mm) in diameter, on the work surface and flatten it slightly.

2. Place one five-card stack of playing cards on each side of the flattened lump and, working with the roller, roll the lump into a sheet, level with height of the cards.

3. With a circle cutter, cut a circle from the metal clay sheet, with the diameter larger than the outside diameter of the neck tube by at least 1/8" (3 mm) all around.

4. Cut a hole in the center of the circle with a smaller circle cutter, with the diameter slightly smaller than the outside diameter of the neck tube.

5. Set the neck lip aside on the mug warmer to dry. When dry, sand and refine the surfaces and edges with salon boards. You'll attach the neck lip to the top end of the neck after the body, neck, and neck collar have been assembled.

ASSEMBLING THE VESSEL BODY

1. When the domes and neck are dry, check the fit of the #1 dome to the #2 dome. Sand the edges of the domes so that they are flat and meet without any gaps.

   To sand the edges, place the dome on the emery paper on a flat surface and move the dome lightly back, forth, and around the emery paper. Do not push down hard! Unfired metal clay is somewhat fragile and could snap if you push too hard. Brush excess sanding dust from the domes with a dry paintbrush.

2. Hold the vessel domes together. Working with a moistened color or clay shaper, salon boards, and the art knife, slowly and carefully refine the opening for the neck tube. Insert the neck tube periodically to confirm the fit. The opening in the vessel body does not have to fit the neck tube perfectly. There can be gaps; they'll be filled in a later step.

3. With the syringe, apply a substantial coil of slip along the edge of one of the domes. You should use more slip than you think you need, so work without the fine syringe tip in place.

4. Gently press the edges of the two domes together, adjusting the fit as you press and allowing some of the slip to ooze out (E). You can smooth some of this away now, but you can also wait until it's dry to sand it down.

5. Set the joined domes on the mug warmer and allow the body to dry completely.

6. When dry, check for gaps in the joint and fill with fresh clay. Dry again.

7. Aggressively sand the joint until you have removed all evidence of the seam and any excess slip. Sand with successively finer grit salon boards or emery paper. Smooth any glaring bumps or creases with a moistened shaper.

E. Join the two domes by gently pressing to form the body of the vessel.

JOINING THE NECK TO THE BODY

1. Sand the seam and the ends of the neck tube. Insert the neck tube into the opening in the vessel body. If the stick is still in the neck, insert the section of the neck that extends beyond the stick into the opening.

2. Adjust the fit of the neck. If the neck is too large, very gently and slowly sand the end of the neck with a salon board until you can insert it smoothly. If it's much too small, coat it with a layer of slip around the end that will be inserted in the opening in the vessel body. Then wrap a thin layer of metal clay sheet (rolled about two cards thick) around the coated area. Allow it to dry and adjust the fit by sanding.

3. When the fit seems good, remove the neck from the domes. Add slip to the end of the neck tube that will be inserted into the vessel body and add slip to the edges of the body opening.

4. Insert the neck tube into the opening in the vessel body. Check to make sure the neck is sitting straight in the opening. Check for any gaps around the joint and fill them with fresh PMC3. Check for any gaps where the domes are joined and fill them also, smoothing with a shaper. Set the parts aside to dry on a mug warmer.

5. When the parts are dry, gently sand and refine, removing all the excess PMC3 slip. Check for any gaps and fill them, using water, slip, and/or fresh PMC3 (depending on the size of the gap).

F. Slide the neck collar into place so it rests snugly on the vessel body.

G. Attach the neck lip by adding slip to the wet side and positioning until secure.

FORMING AND JOINING THE VESSEL COLLAR

1. The neck collar will be attached at the shoulder of the vessel body where the neck and the vessel body meet. Select two circle cutters—one should just fit around the neck of the vessel and the other should be a little larger. Oil one end of each circle cutter.

2. Roll out a sheet of PMC3, three cards thick, on the work surface.

3. With the smaller circle cutter, punch out one hole in the PMC3 sheet.

4. With the larger circle cutter, punch out a flattened doughnut shape centered around the previously punched hole.

5. Slide this collar down the neck to the vessel body and bend and drape it so it conforms to the shape of the vessel body (**F**). Place the body on the mug warmer to dry.

6. When the collar is dry, remove it from the body. (It's removable because the body was dry when the collar was draped and there was no slip added.)

7. Add slip to the concave side of the collar and slide it down the neck again. Press it onto the body of the vessel.

8. When the collar is dry, check for gaps and fill them with slip, smoothing it into the gaps with a shaper.

JOINING NECK LIP TO THE NECK

1. Wet one side of the neck lip and the top edge of the neck. Add slip to the wet side of the neck lip.

2. Place the neck lip onto the top of the neck, rotating a little to secure it (**G**).

3. Set the parts aside to dry. Then, sand and refine all the edges, adding slip or fresh PMC3 if there are gaps, especially in the opening at the top of the neck. Rotate a moistened shaper in the opening to round the opening if needed and to smooth any bumps or flaws.

FORMING THE SPIRALS

1. The spirals require a very delicate touch—but don't let this discourage you from making them. (If you don't want to try making the spirals, however, skip this entire section and go to Making the Hole Supports, page 123, to continue.)

    The spirals can be made in one of two ways. They can be either hand-cut or they can be made with an extruder. The extruder guarantees an even, smooth strip of metal clay.

    If you are using the extruder, oil the parts and one die that has a single narrow rectangular hole, about 1/8" (3 mm) wide. Assemble the extruder and continue to step 2. If you don't want to use an extruder, skip to step 3.

2. Remove a small lump of PMC3 from the package. Make sure the PMC3 is relatively moist (add a little water if cracks appear when it's pressed between the fingers). Place a lump of PMC3 in the extruder. Extrude a flat strip. Cut two lengths from the strip, each about 2" (5 cm) long.

H. Form spirals from strips made by hand or with an extruder.

3. If you're not using an extruder, roll out a metal clay sheet to two cards thick. Use the tissue blade to cut two strips, about ⅛" (3 mm) wide and 2" (5 cm) long.

4. Trim the ends of each strip with a tissue blade, forming a tapered tip.

5. Roll each of the tips into small, tight coils and form the strips into matching S shapes (**H**). Place the pieces on the mug warmer to dry completely.

6. When the pieces are dry, place one flat on a fine-grit salon board and very gently sand it so that it is completely flat. Repeat the sanding process with the second spiral.

JOINING THE SPIRALS TO THE VESSEL

1. Use slip to join the spirals to each other, using the vessel body as a guide (**I**). Join at an angle that will match the curve at the bottom of the vessel body.

2. Place the spirals on a flat surface and hold them together for 30 seconds. Then place them on the mug warmer to dry completely.

3. Bend the copper screen into a form that will support the vessel body vertically and when turned upside down.

4. Hold the joined spirals against the bottom of the vessel body and check to see where they touch the body. Add slip to those points of contact. Press the spirals against the body and hold for 30 seconds (**J**).

5. Place the vessel upside down in the copper support and set the support directly on the mug warmer until the joints are completely dry (**K**). (You can speed the drying with a handheld hair dryer while the vessel is on the mug warmer.)

6. When the spiral joints are dry, check for gaps and add a little water, slip, and fresh PMC3 where necessary.

7. Set the piece aside on the warmer to dry again.

8. When the joints are dry, remove the excess slip with salon boards and the art knife. Work very gently and, if needed, use your fingers to support the spirals underneath the area that is being worked on. Smooth and refine the joints with a moistened shaper.

I. Join the S shapes with slip to a curve that conforms to the vessel bottom.

J. Attach the spirals to the vessel by adding slip to the points of contact.

K. The copper support holds the vessel in position while it's drying on the mug warmer.

L. Add slip to the concave side of the hole support and seat it on the dry shoulder of the vessel.

MAKING THE HOLE SUPPORTS

1. Place a lump of metal clay about ¼" (6–7 mm) in diameter on the work surface. Place one three-card stack of cards on either side of the metal clay. Working with the roller, roll the metal clay into a sheet, three-cards thick.

2. With the tissue blade, cut one small shape about 1½" (3.8 cm) square. Lift it from the work surface, using the tissue blade, and drape it on the "shoulder" of the vessel.

3. Place the vessel in the copper support on the mug warmer, resting with the square hole support facing up. Dry completely.

4. Remove the hole support from the vessel and add slip to the concave side of it. Press it against the "shoulder" where it dried (**L**). Smooth any excess slip that oozes out of the joint.

5. Repeat steps 1–4 for the second hole support, placing it on the opposite "shoulder" of the vessel.

6. Moisten a spot in the center of one of the hole supports and scratch a small depression in that spot with the scribe.

7. If you haven't already decided how to suspend your bead, make that decision now. For example, you can thread the bead on silk cord, leather thong, silver chain, or ribbon. Your choice will determine the size of the hole required. Select the size drill bit that will make the appropriate hole size.

8. Gently rest the vessel bead on a clean work surface with the moistened hole support facing up.

9. Stabilize the bead with one hand and rest the drill bit in the depression.

10. Without pressing too hard, rotate the drill bit, cutting into the surface of the hole support. You'll know that the drill bit is rotating in the correct direction when you see small curved bits of dried metal clay exiting the hole.

11. Carefully drill through the hole support and the vessel, allowing the drill bit to do its job, without putting too much pressure on it. In this "greenware" state, your bead is somewhat fragile and too much pressure could crack it.

12. When the drill bit has broken through to the interior of the vessel, continue rotating the drill while slipping it back out of the hole.

13. Repeat steps 6–12 to drill through the second hole support.

14. Moisten the edges of the hole. Then countersink the hole opening by gently rotating the large drill bit in the moistened metal clay a few turns, until there is a visible tapered edge. Do not drill through to the inside of the bead as this will eliminate the taper/countersink. Countersinking creates a tapered edge on the hole opening, allowing the bead to swing easily when suspended—especially useful with a large bead like this vessel bead. If the holes have any ragged edges, twirl a moistened color shaper in the holes to smooth the edges. Set aside to dry again.

15. Sand and refine any irregularities, check for gaps, and fill with slip or fresh PMC3. Dry completely.

M. Press the bezel cup into the surface of the metal clay square.

N. Position the bezel cup unit on the surface of the vessel, pressing gently to confirm the joint.

THE BEZEL UNIT

1. Oil the work surface, the tissue blade, the roller, the shaper, and your hands.

2. Roll out a sheet of metal clay about four cards thick and trim it to ³⁄₈" to ½" (9 to 12 mm) square.

3. Gently press the bezel cup into the surface, allowing some of the metal clay to ooze through the opening and into the cup. Leave some of the top edge of the bezel cup above the surface of the square (**M**). If you'd like, use a scribe or steel punch to add decorative marks around the bezel cup on the surface of the square.

4. Rest the bezel cup unit on the surface of the vessel, gently bending it to match the curve of the vessel, and place the vessel on the mug warmer to dry.

5. If you want to set the bead with a cabochon on both sides, repeat steps 1–4 now.

6. When the bezel cup unit is dry, sand all the edges of the metal clay.

7. Join the unit to one side of the vessel bead using a little water and enough slip to make a solid joint (**N**). If you made a second bezel cup unit, join it to the vessel, too. Check for any gaps or flaws and repair them now.

8. Dry the bead on the mug warmer. With a moistened shaper, salon boards, the art knife, and Tri-M-Ite Sheets, refine and smooth the joints and surfaces of the vessel bead.

FIRING THE VESSEL BEAD

1. Put on a respirator or good dust mask and vinyl gloves. Fill the fireproof container with alumina hydrate.

2. Place the bead on the alumina hydrate. Then place the container on a firing surface, kiln pad, or firebrick in a cold kiln. Close the kiln door.

3. Turn on the kiln and select the program that will allow the kiln to run for 2 hours at 900°C/1650°F. Even though PMC3 can fire at lower temperatures, this firing schedule produces a stronger bead.

4. After the kiln has completed the firing cycle, allow it to cool down a little and open the door to allow it to cool down even more.

5. Check the digital readout of the temperature on the kiln and, after the kiln has cooled down, using the tweezers and wearing the gloves, move the bead to another fireproof surface to air-cool, or quench it in a large stainless-steel bowl filled with cool water.

6. Finish and polish bead (see page 25).

O. The bezel is pressed against the stone at the four cardinal points: north, south, east, and west.

SETTING THE GEMSTONE

1. In these next steps, you'll push the bezel against the stone at each of the four cardinal points (north, south, east, and west, in that order). Drop the stone into the bezel cup. Holding the bead steady in one hand, hold the bezel pusher in the other hand and use it to gently push against the top edge of the wall of the bezel cup, pressing it against the stone. Don't put excessive pressure on the body of the bead.

2. Rotate the bead and push on the cup at the exact opposite side.

3. Again rotate the bead, but this time only one-quarter of the way around the cup. Press the wall of the bezel once again.

4. Rotate the bead so that you can press the wall on the opposite side you just pressed in step 3 **(O)**.

5. Now begin to press between those points that you have already pressed, continuing to move the bezel pusher to opposite locations.

6. Roll the bezel pusher around the edge of the bezel wall, smoothing any little kinks that might have developed and compressing any spots you might have missed in the previous steps.

7. Vigorously rub around the edge of the bezel cup with the polishing cloth.

ARTIST: CeCe Wire
MATERIALS: fine silver, cubic zirconium
TECHNIQUES: metal clay, pavé setting of faceted cubic zirconium, stone setting with bur-made depressions and metal clay paste
DIMENSIONS: 1" (2.5 cm) diameter

photo: Robert Diamante

Fitting the Stone in the Cup

After you have completed the polishing and finishing of the bead, it's time to set the gemstone. Place a length of dental floss across the bezel cup and drop the stone in the cup. The walls of the cup should capture just the barest edge of the stone's girdle—the widest part of the stone. If the stone rests too deeply in the cup, you may have to add a little lift. If so, remove the stone from the cup, using the dental floss to help remove it.

A number of materials can be used to supply lift: multiple pieces of aluminum foil; precious metal sheet (fine silver or sterling work well); fine sawdust; clear, water-based caulking, to name a few. If your stone is transparent or translucent, aluminum foil or fine silver sheet will provide the best solution.

Cut a piece of lift material equal to the size of the bezel cup and test the stone height again with the help of dental floss. Keep testing until, when you look at the bezel cup from the side, the walls are just high enough to capture the girdle of the gemstone. Lift out the stone and remove the floss.

Sometimes, fingers just seem to be too large and clumsy when handling small stones. Instead, use a little ball of sticky wax to lift the stone and place it in the setting.

Gallery of Artists' METAL CLAY Beads

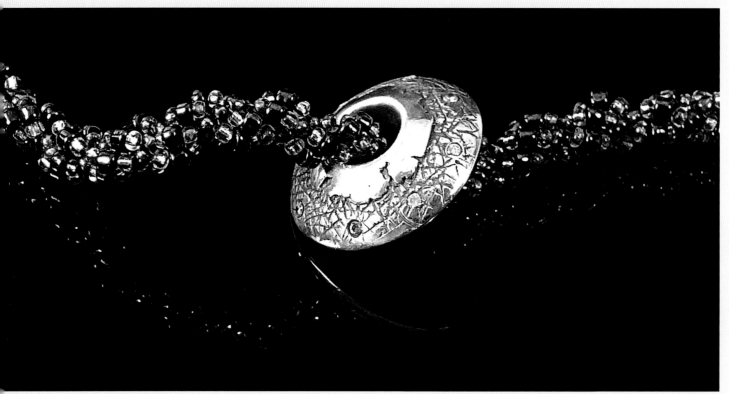

photo: Maggie Bergman

Disk Bead

ARTIST: Maggie Bergman
MATERIALS: fine silver, cubic zirconia
TECHNIQUES: metal clay, dry construction, stone setting
DIMENSIONS: 1⅛" × ½" (28 mm × 13 mm)

Congo Bead

ARTIST: Maggie Bergman
MATERIALS: fine silver, leather, glass
TECHNIQUES: metal clay, Cork Clay construction
DIMENSIONS: ⅝" × 1¼" (8.3 cm × 2 cm)

Mika

ARTIST: Gwen Bernecker
MATERIALS: fine silver, 24k gold keum-boo
TECHNIQUES: hollow form construction, patination
DIMENSIONS: 2" × 1¼" × ⅝" (50 mm × 30 mm × 16 mm)

Now Paint the Town Red

ARTIST: Angela Baduel-Crispin
MATERIALS: fine and sterling silver, faux bone, silk bristles
TECHNIQUES: PMC3, core-formed, carved, patination, polishing
DIMENSIONS: 3" high × 1" wide × 2³⁄₈" deep (7.5 cm × 2.5 cm × 6 cm)

Cloud Forest Pocketbook

ARTIST: Jean Wydra

MATERIALS: fine silver

TECHNIQUES: metal clay, wet construction over wax-coated foam core, hard-wire bezels mounted in wet clay, secondary beads formed with syringe

DIMENSIONS: central bead 2¾" high × 1" wide × 1" deep (68 mm × 25 mm × 25 mm)

photo: Larry Sanders

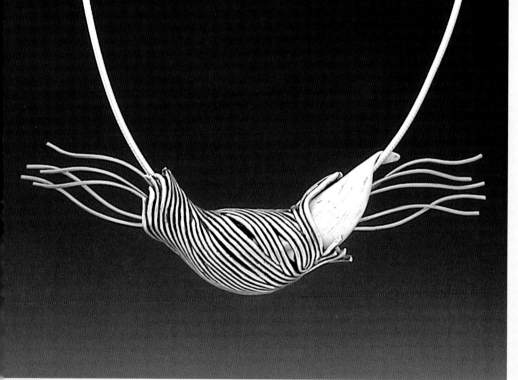

photo: Angela Baduel-Crispin

Fly...No Strings Attached

ARTIST: Angela Baduel-Crispin

MATERIALS: fine and sterling silver, faux bone, copper

TECHNIQUES: metal clay, extrusion, riveting, patination, polishing

DIMENSIONS: 4⅞" wide × ½" deep (125 mm × 13 mm)

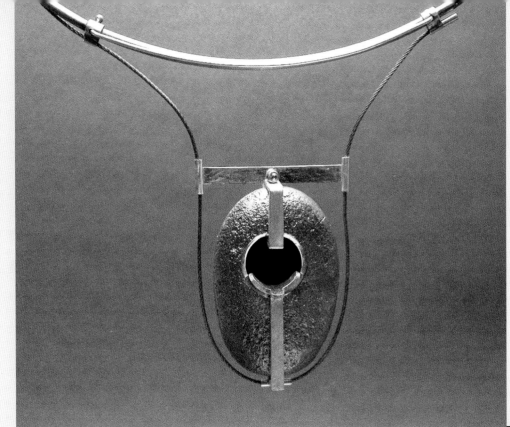

photo: Chet Bolins

Bronze Clay Pebble Necklace

ARTIST: Chris Darway
MATERIALS: bronze, titanium, sterling silver, 14k gold, stainless-steel cable
TECHNIQUES: bronze metal clay, two-piece RTV rubber mold, traditional metalworking techniques
DIMENSIONS: 11" × 8" (28 cm × 20 cm)

Mesh Rectangle Bead

ARTIST: Chris Darway
MATERIALS: fine silver, sterling silver
TECHNIQUES: PMC+, fine silver mesh, sterling silver tubing fired with PMC+ at a firing temperature of 1470°F (800°C) for 30 minutes (sterling is black from oxidation)
DIMENSIONS: 2" long × ³⁄₈" diameter (50 mm × 9.5 mm)

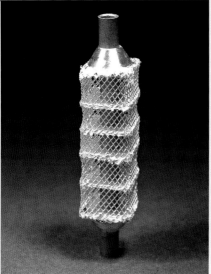

photo: Chet Bolins

photo: Chet Bolins

Mesh Cylinder Bead

ARTIST: Chris Darway
MATERIALS: fine silver, sterling silver
TECHNIQUES: PMC+, fine silver mesh, sterling silver tubing fired with PMC+ at a firing temperature of 1470°F (800°C) for 30 minutes (sterling is black from oxidation)
DIMENSIONS: 2" long × ³⁄₈" diameter (50 mm × 9.5 mm)

Photo: Drew Davidson

Mio Dolce Amore
(Love Letter Series)

ARTIST: Tonya Davidson

MATERIALS: fine silver, precious stones, pearls, glass

TECHNIQUES: press-molded, veneer, carved, textured, stone setting (pressed and syringe-set), brass-brushed, wheel-polished, patination

DIMENSIONS: focal piece 1¼" diameter × ¼" deep (32 mm × 7 mm)

Photo: Drew Davidson

My Lord and Dear Husband
(Love Letter Series)

ARTIST: Tonya Davidson

MATERIALS: fine silver, opal

TECHNIQUES: texturing, veneer, press-molded, carved, bezel stone setting, brass-brushed, wheel-polished

DIMENSIONS: 1³/₁₆" diameter × ⁵/₁₆" deep (30 mm × 8 mm)

Photo: Drew Davidson

A Thousand Kisses
(Love Letter Series)

ARTIST: Tonya Davidson

MATERIALS: fine silver, sapphires

TECHNIQUES: textured, syringe and paste design, veneer, syringe and pressed stone setting

DIMENSIONS: 1⅝" high × ¾" wide × ⅜" deep (40 mm × 19 mm × 9 mm)

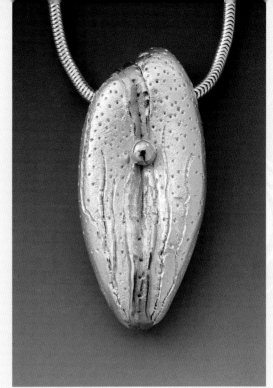

Pod Bead Pendant

ARTIST: Nancy Karpel

MATERIALS: fine and stering silver, 24k and 18k gold

TECHNIQUES: metal clay, hollow form construction (wax core), 18k gold soldered on after firing

DIMENSIONS: central bead 1½" high × 4½" wide × ¼" deep (38 mm × 116 mm × 6 mm)

photo: Frank Poole

Ancient Writing

ARTIST: Pat Gullett

MATERIAL: fine silver

TECHNIQUES: metal clay, hollow form construction (Cork Clay core), photopolymer plate texture

DIMENSIONS: 1⅛" (28 mm) square

photo: Doug Foulkes Photography

photo: Evan J. Soldinger

Dreaming the Sea

ARTIST: Linda Kaye-Moses

MATERIALS: fine silver, silk, tourmaline, beryl, chrysoprase

TECHNIQUES: printing block carving, dry hollow form construction, printing, draping, patination, riveting, postfiring stone setting

DIMENSIONS: total length 16" (41 cm), 8 bead pendants 1⁷⁄₁₆" high × ½" wide × ⅕" deep (36 mm × 12 mm × 5 mm), central bead pendant 1¹⁵⁄₁₆" high × ½" wide × ⁷⁄₃₂" deep (49 mm × 12 mm × 5 mm)

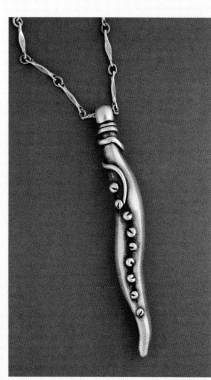

photo: Jeanette Landenwitch

Pendant Bead

ARTIST: Jeanette Landenwitch

MATERIAL: fine silver

TECHNIQUES: hollow form construction (core removed before firing), patination

DIMENSIONS: PMC bead 2½" (6 cm) long, total length 17" (43 cm) long

Botanicals

ARTIST: Terry Kovalcik

MATERIAL: fine silver

TECHNIQUES: PMC+, PMC3 paste, hollow form construction; painting, patination

DIMENSIONS: 5/8" (16 mm) high

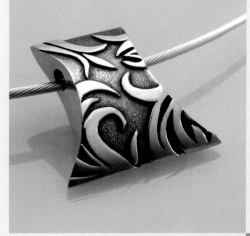

photo: Corrin Jacobsen Kovalcik

photo: Corrin Jacobsen Kovalcik

Graduated Bead Necklace

ARTIST: Jeanette Landenwitch

MATERIALS: fine silver, onyx, sterling

TECHNIQUES: metal clay, hollow form construction, wire-brushed, stippled

DIMENSIONS: total length 18" (45.7 cm) long

photo: Jeanette Landenwitch

Graphic Swirls

ARTIST: Terry Kovalcik

MATERIAL: fine silver

TECHNIQUES: PMC+, PMC3 paste, painting, patination

DIMENSIONS: 1 3/8" (35 mm) high

photo: Larry Sanders

Necklace

ARTIST: Candice Wakumoto

MATERIALS: fine and sterling silver, 22k and 18k gold, boulder opal, turquoise, apatite

TECHNIQUES: hollow core contruction (cork clay), keum-boo

DIMENSIONS: 1¾" × 2" (45 mm × 50 mm)

In the Jungle

ARTIST: Jeanette Landenwitch

MATERIALS: bronze, turquoise, gold-filled beads

TECHNIQUES: bronze metal clay (hollow and solid)

DIMENSIONS: total length 7" (43 cm) long

photo: Jeanette Landenwitch

Set of Nine Beads

ARTIST: Wendy Malinow

MATERIALS: fine silver, polymer clay

TECHNIQUES: hollow form construction, patination, PMC3, polymer clay inlay

DIMENSIONS: 1½"–3" (38–76 mm) long

photo: Courtney Frisse

photo: Robert Diamante

Bead

ARTIST: CeCe Wire

MATERIALS: fine silver, vitreous enamels

TECHNIQUES: metal clay, wet-pack enameling, water-etching

DIMENSIONS: 1" (2.5 cm) diameter

Set of Four Beads

ARTIST: Wendy Malinow

MATERIALS: fine silver, polymer clay

TECHNIQUES: hollow core construction, PMC3, polymer clay inlay, patina

DIMENSIONS: 1¼"–4" (32–100 mm) long

photo: Courtney Frisse

Spine

ARTIST: Wendy Malinow

MATERIAL: fine silver

TECHNIQUES: hollow form construction, patination, PMC3

DIMENSIONS: 25" (63.5 cm) long

photo: Courtney Frisse

Collage 1

ARTIST: Barbara Becker Simon

MATERIALS: fine silver, porphery, glass, granite, stainless steel, sterling silver

TECHNIQUES: hollow form construction, patination

DIMENSIONS: 18" (45.7 cm) long

photo: Larry Sanders

Focal Point

ARTIST: Catherine Davies Paetz
MATERIALS: fine silver, leather
TECHNIQUES: hollow form dry construction
DIMENSIONS: 1³⁄₈" high × ⁵⁄₈" wide × ⁷⁄₁₆" deep (35 mm × 17 mm × 11 mm)

photo: Catherine Davies Paetz

Bead

ARTIST: CeCe Wire
MATERIALS: fine silver, cubic zirconium grit, Prismacolor pencil
TECHNIQUES: metal clay, cubic zirconium grit pressed into wet metal clay and applied to the bead surface, colored pencil coloring of bead surface
DIMENSIONS: 1" (2.5 cm) diameter

Ant Lentil

ARTIST: Barbara Becker Simon
MATERIALS: fine silver, 22k gold, diamonds
TECHNIQUES: hollow form construction, patination
DIMENSIONS: 1" (25 mm) diameter

photo: Babette Belmondo

photo: Robert Diamante

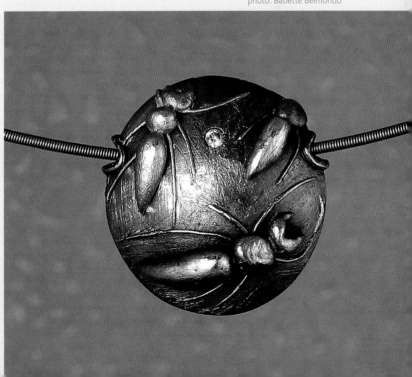

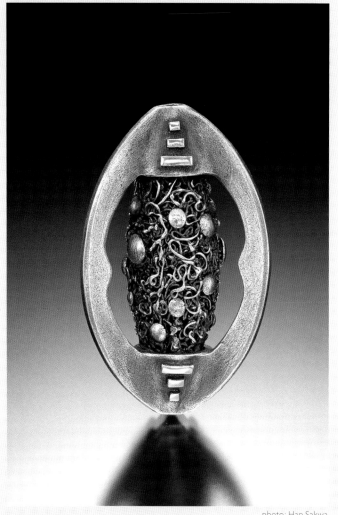

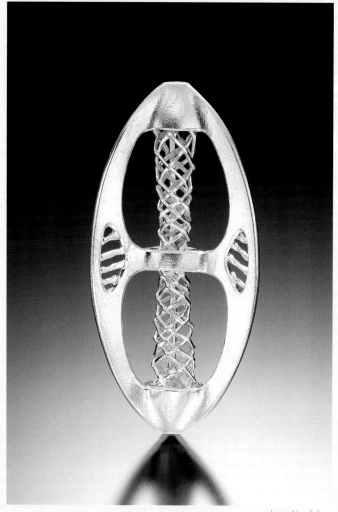

photo: Hap Sakwa

photo: Hap Sakwa

Alien Bead #2

ARTIST: Gordon Uyehara
MATERIAL: fine silver (Art Clay)
TECHNIQUES: syringe, burnable core, stenciled, fired vertically in fiber blanket
DIMENSIONS: 1½" × 1" (39 mm × 24 mm)

Silver Interlude

ARTIST: Gordon Uyehara
MATERIALS: fine silver (Art Clay)
TECHNIQUES: syringe, burnable core, rolled, stenciled
DIMENSIONS: 2³⁄₈" × 1¹⁄₈" (61 mm × 29 mm)

Cousin, Brother

ARTIST: Jean Wydra

MATERIALS: fine silver, rhodocrosite, kyanite

TECHNIQUES: metal clay, wet construction over wax-coated foam core, hard wire bezels mounted in wet clay, secondary beads formed with syringe

DIMENSIONS: central bead 2" high × 1½" wide × 1½" deep (50 mm × 38 mm × 38 mm)

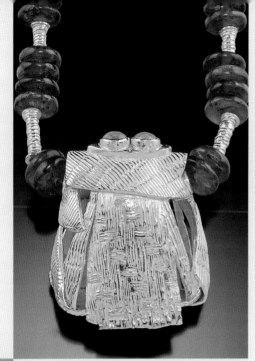

photo: Larry Sanders

photo: Eleanor Moty

Necklace

ARTIST: Eleanor Moty

MATERIALS: fine silver, quartz, moonstone, pearls

TECHNIQUES: hollow form construction (Sculptamold), PMC Standard

DIMENSIONS: PMC bead 2¾" × ½" (6.9 cm × 1.3 cm), total length 26" (66 cm)

Necklace

ARTIST: Candice Wakumoto
MATERIALS: fine and sterling silver,
24k gold, turquoise, lava, vermeil
TECHNIQUES: hollow form construction
(Cork Clay core), fabricated bezel
DIMENSIONS: 1¾" × 2" (45 mm × 50 mm)

photo: Larry Sanders

Profundo

ARTIST: Marco Fleseri
MATERIALS: fine silver and fresh-water pearls
TECHNIQUES: metal clay, hollow form construction, hand-sculpted, Cork Clay core (cured several days), paste-painted with added design elements, air- and heat-dried (hair dryer)
DIMENSIONS: 18" (45.7 cm) long

photo: Marco Fleseri

photo: Marco Fleseri

Laguna

ARTIST: Marco Fleseri
MATERIALS: fine silver, fluorite, turquoise
TECHNIQUES: metal clay, hollow form construction, hand-sculpted, Cork Clay core (cured for several days), paste-painted with added design elements; air- and heat-dried (hair dryer)
DIMENSIONS: 18" (45.7 cm) long

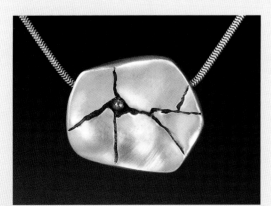

photo: Hadar Jacobson

Lost

ARTIST: Hadar Jacobson
MATERIALS: fine silver, natural sapphire
TECHNIQUES: hollow form construction (Cork Clay core), stone fired in place
DIMENSIONS: 1 1/8" × 3/4" × 1/8" (30 mm × 20 mm × 5 mm)

Glossary

Acrylic medium: a pastelike acrylic formula ordinarily used to manipulate acrylic colors; used to make printing plates for metal clay

Active ventilation: the removal of the smoke and fumes from firing and other processes by positioning a fan that will not draw the fumes past your nose, but will instead vent the smoke and fumes away from you and to the outside

Armature: a support for a metal clay bead during construction and/or firing

Binder: the claylike material in which the precious metal particles are embedded

Burnishing: compressing the surface of metal to achieve a bright, smooth look

Cabochon: an unfaceted, convex-cut gemstone

Casting wax: wax that is generally used to make models for reproduction of metal objects; used with metal clay to support hollow beads or other hollow forms

Circle cutters: small metal cutters, like miniature cookie cutters, for cutting regular shapes out of metal clay; available in graduated sizes; generally made of brass

Circle template: clear plastic sheet with open, graduated circles; used with a needle tool or scribe to draw and cut circles on metal clay

Copper mesh screen: coarse copper mesh used on a mug warmer to support drying metal clay pieces

Core: the interior support or framework for a metal clay bead during construction and/or while it is being fired.

Dehydrator: originally designed for drying vegetables and other foods; useful for quickly drying large quantities of metal clay objects

Emery paper: abrasive paper in a range of grits; can be used for sanding unfired and sintered metal clay

Extender: an additive for extending the drying time of metal clay (see Glycerin)

Extruder: a small tube into which metal clay is placed and pressed or extruded through a die to create specific shapes

Fine silver: the unalloyed form of silver; referred to as .999 parts silver

Firing temperature: the temperature(s) at which each formula of metal clay must be fired to sinter the metal particles

Firing time: the minimum amount of time at which each formula of metal clay must be fired to sinter the metal particles

Flexible shaft machine or flex shaft: an electric rotary machine comprised of a motor, a rheostat/foot pedal (for governing speed), a hand piece, and a flexible shaft (connecting the motor to the hand piece); used with a variety of wheels and bits for a drilling, polishing, and grinding. (This tool and all rotary tools should always be used with safety goggles or face shield and a dust mask or respirator. Remove all jewelry and tie back hair before using this machine.)

Girdle: the widest part of a gemstone, located at the base of a cabochon stone

Glycerin: a clear, colorless, viscous liquid belonging to the alcohol family of organic compounds; used to slow the drying of metal clay and to make metal clay sheet that remains somewhat flexible

Grit: the fineness or coarseness of various sanding or finishing materials (see emery paper, salon boards, and Scotch-Brite)

Hydrate: to remoisten partially or completely dried metal clay.

Jewelry stamp/leather stamp or punch: metal tool for applying designs to metal clay

Kiln: a small furnace used for sintering metal clay, generally computer controlled

Kiln, trinket: a small tabletop kiln capable of firing metal clay and enamels, among other tasks

Kiln, Ultralite: a trademarked trinket kiln used for metal clay, fusing fine silver, enameling, and glass fusing

Letterpress ornaments: originally used by printers and useful for stamping designs into a metal clay surface or element; available in online auctions and antique shops

Liver of sulfur: a chemical used to darken or patinate fine silver, sterling silver, and copper (see Patina/Patination)

Lubrication: here achieved with olive oil, used to prevent metal clay from adhering to hands, tools, and surfaces

Microfinishing papers: micron fine abrasives mounted on a paperlike backing; used for hand-finishing precious and nonprecious metals

Mister: a small bottle for spraying water in mistlike droplets; used for rehydrating partially dry metal clay

Mold: the frame or cavity in which unfired metal clay is pressed to give it a decorative shape

Mold-making materials: materials that can be used to make molds for metal clay

Needle tool: a large sewing needle used to work metal clay

Oxides: matte white deposits of fine silver on the surface of just-fired metal clay

Patina/Patination: a chemically produced surface coloration of metal

Press-molded: soft material, such as metal clay, pressed into a mold to reproduce an image or form

Quenching: placing fired, hot metal clay objects immediately from the kiln into cold water in a heatproof container (such as stainless steel) to cool off quickly

Rehydrating: the addition of water to partially or completely dry metal clay to restore it to workable form

Roller: small plastic tube or rod (such as PVC pipe or Plexiglas) used to roll out metal clay sheet

Rotary tool: an electric tool into which is installed a range of polishing, drilling, and grinding wheels (see Flexible-shaft machine)

Salon boards: narrow sanding boards in a range of grits, originally designed for finishing artificial fingernails, but useful for sanding unfired and sintered metal clay

Scotch-Brite: a trademarked abrasive, useful for finishing metal surfaces. Available in several grits, it can be purchased in different forms: 6"× 6" (15 × 15 cm) square pads or mounted on mandrels for rotary tools

Scribe: a sharp-pointed tool for making marks and/or cleaning off excess metal clay or slip

Shapers: paintbrush-type tools with a solid rubberlike tip; used to move and smooth metal clay and slip; available in assorted sizes, shapes, and hardnesses

Sintering: the process where the precious metal particles in metal clay bond without melting; accomplished by heating to a specific temperature for specific length of time

Slip: a more fluid, thinner form of metal clay; used to join metal clay parts, for slip-painting, or for repairs

Slip-painting: the application of many layers of slip to the surface of a supporting model

Sunshine cloth: one of many different types of polishing cloths; used for final finishing step for precious metal

Thickness guides: spacers, slats, playing cards used to roll out metal clay sheet to a predetermined thickness

3M Scotch-Brite Radial Bristle Discs: a trademarked abrasive-coated, plastic brushlike wheel for use with rotary tools; available in a range of grits

Tissue blade: extremely sharp, long rectangular slicing tool

Torch-firing: using a torch to fire metal clay, an alternative to kiln-firing, requiring continuous attention and monitoring

Vitreous enamel: opaque or transparent extremely fine colored glass granules; applied to the surface of metal objects and then fired

Waterbrush: a narrow plastic cylinder capable of holding and dispensing water through a brush on one end

Wood Clay: a trademarked, compressed, nontoxic byproduct of the pencil-making industry that can be shaped, dried, covered with metal clay, and fired in a kiln; used to form bead cores or armatures

Work Surface: the immediate surface on which to form metal clay objects

Worktable: the table or workbench on which the work surface and other tools are placed

Appendices

PMC FORMULAS

The firing temperatures and durations listed here are those recommended by Mitsubishi Materials of Japan, the manufacturer of Precious Metal Clay (PMC):

The ratio of fine silver to binder in PMC+ and PMC3 are the same. The difference in density between the two formulas results from the different sizes of the metal particles in the clay.

The melting point of fine silver is 1762°F (960°C), much higher than the firing temperatures for any of the Precious Metal Clay formulas. When PMC is fired to the correct temperatures, there is no danger of melting the object being fired. All formulas of PMC can be fired to 1650°F (900°C) without interfering with the sintering process.

	Firing Temperature and Duration	Form(s)	Shrinkage	Percentages	Metal Particles	Cost	Density
Formula: PMC Standard (Precious Metal Clay, also known as PMC Original)	1650°F (900°C) for 2 hours	Lump only	+/– 28%	80% fine silver, 20% water and binder	largest, irregular in shape	Least expensive	Lowest
	Comment: Easy to handle, dries more slowly, and takes textures beautifully. Because of the greater shrinkage, any texture becomes more pronounced, more intense. The strength is not as dense as the other two silver formulas, so it's not as suitable for some projects, such as bracelets or rings, although it can be adapted to those objects when necessary.						
Formula: PMC+ (Precious Metal Clay Plus)	1470°F (800°C) for 30 minutes; 1560°F (850°C) for 20 minutes; 1650°F (900°C) for 10 minutes	Lump, slip in jar, slip in syringe, paper/sheet	12–15%	90% fine silver, 10% water and binder	Smaller than PMC Standard, spherical, various sizes	More expensive than Original and less expensive than PMC3	More dense than Original and less dense than PMC3
	Comment: I prefer to work with PMC3 for strength. PMC+, though, is somewhat stronger than PMC Standard and can be made slightly stronger with the hotter/longer firing.						

PMC FORMULAS (CONT.)

	Firing Temperature and Duration	Form(s)	Shrinkage	Percentages	Metal Particles	Cost	Density
Formula: PMC3 (Precious Metal Clay 3)	1110°F (600°C) for 45 minutes; 1200°F (650°C) for 20 minutes; 1290°F (700°C) for 10 minutes	Lump, slip in jar, slip in syringe	12–15%	90% fine silver 10% water and Binder	Smallest of the three fine silver formulas; different sizes; spherical	Most expensive of the fine silver PMC formulas	Most dense of the three fine silver products
	Comment: Preferred for objects that require strength and can be made slightly stronger with the hotter/longer firing; can be torch fired.						
Formula: 22k Yellow Gold PMC	1290°F (700°C) for 90 minutes; 1380°F (750°C) for 60 minutes; 1560°F (850°C) for 30 minutes, 1650°F (900°C) for 10 minutes	Lump only	12–15%	91.7% pure gold, 8.3% silver, water, and binder	spherical, different sizes	Most expensive Precious Metal Clay	Relatively dense and strong
	Comment: Very beautiful gold; most practical when combined with silver formulas (Some of the temperatures overlap with the temperatures of the silver formulas, so they can be fired together.)						

FIRING SURFACES AND KILN FURNITURE

	Cost	Convenience	Durability	Availability
Soft Firebrick	Least expensive	Must be cut into ⅝" (16 mm) -thick slabs; creates dust (so requires user to wear a good dust mask/respirator), will stack	Eventually breaks, but pieces can still be used; can be stacked	Pottery suppliers
Asbestos-free Soldering Pads	Reasonable	Will fit in kilns without cutting to size	Longer lasting than firebrick, but eventually breaks (pieces can still be used); will stack	Jewelry-making suppliers
Pottery/Ceramic Kiln Furniture	Most expensive	Sizes available for kiln dimensions; many different shapes available; will stack	Most durable	Pottery/ceramic suppliers

FIRING CONTAINERS

Firing containers, or saggers, and the materials they contain (vermiculite, alumina hydrate, sand), are used to support beads and other curved or hollow metal clay forms during the firing process. They help to prevent slumping or collapsing of the beads under their own weight.

Firing containers/saggers can be any type of container or box that is heat-resistant (up to 1650°F [900°C]), such as small stainless-steel bowls, small terra-cotta flowerpots, and terra-cotta flowerpot saucers. If a metal container is not marked as stainless steel, it is probably aluminum, and cannot be used for this task.

SUPPORT MATERIALS

None of the various heat-resistant support materials used in saggers is perfect. The following materials all have a melting temperature much higher than the temperatures used for firing metal clay.

	Description	Advantages	Disadvantages
Alumina Hydrate	Fine granular white powder about the consistency of talcum powder, made as a glaze additive for potters	Readily available at potter's suppliers; works very well; is reusable an infinite number of times; inexpensive	Available from pottery suppliers; powder becomes airborne and can be inhaled (toxic); recommended that user wear respirator when placing it in the sagger
Vermiculite	Coarse material made from heat-expanded mica	Readily available at garden centers; works very well; is reusable an infinite number of times; very inexpensive	Sometimes leaves marks on the metal clay; powder can become airborne and can be inhaled (toxic); recommended that user wear respirator when placing it in the sagger
Perlite	Inert, heat-expanded, white, granular material derived from volcanic rock	Readily available at garden centers; works very well; is reusable an infinite number of times; very inexpensive	Must be fired at temperatures below 1600°F (870°C); powder can become airborne and can be inhaled (toxic); recommended that user wear respirator when placing it in the sagger
Clay-based Kitty Litter	Granular material sold as absorbent material for cat litter	Readily available at pet supply centers; works very well; is reusable an infinite number of times; very inexpensive	Powder can become airborne and can be inhaled; recommended that user wear respirator when placing it in the sagger
Silica Potter's Sand	Silica-based sand	Works very well; is reusable an infinite number of times; relatively inexpensive	Only available from pottery suppliers; powder can become airborne and can be inhaled; recommended that user wear respirator when placing it in the sagger
Kaowool	Fiberglass high-temperature insulation material	Works very well for this purpose; is reusable an infinite number of times; can be used without a container; relatively inexpensive	Must be ordered through the mail (online)

MOLD-MAKING MATERIALS

	Type of Material	Advantages	Disadvantages
Belicold	Two-part silicone	Contains its own release; gives you time (5 to 25 minutes) before it sets up (cures); picks up detail well; durable; resulting mold can be used repeatedly; does not need to be sealed	A little more expensive than other materials; model must remain in material until cured (hard); must be mixed in two equal parts; cannot be remade or "uncured" after curing; not as readily available as other materials; cannot be used to take impression from some rubber stamps or rubber forms
	Comments: Can be ordered from a variety of sources; even though it contains its own release, requires a little olive oil as a mold release when pressing wet PMC into it; store in the dark		
Friendly Plastic	Thermoplastic pellets	Can be reused; requires only hot water to soften or prepare it for use; picks up detail well; does not need to be sealed; very durable; resulting mold can be used repeatedly; no release required to remove the model while making the mold (although I always add just a little olive oil to be on the safe side)	Preparation water must be at least 160°F (71°C); model must remain in material until opaque and hard; not as readily available as some of the other materials; difficult to see whether details have been achieved until metal clay is pressed into it
	Comments: Must be ordered through the mail (online); requires a little olive oil as mold release when pressing wet PMC into it		
Super Sculpey	Polymer clays	Readily available; picks up detail well; model can be removed before curing/baking; very durable; resulting mold can be used repeatedly	Cannot be remade after baking/curing; requires conditioning; requires oven for curing; release required while making the mold from the model (equal parts talcum powder/cornstarch)
	Comments: Requires a little olive oil as mold release when pressing wet PMC into it		
Papier-mâché	paper and various types of additives	Readily available; durable; resulting mold can be used repeatedly; inexpensive	must be sealed (varnish) for use with metal clay; not the best for picking up fine detail; long drying time; messy
	Requires a little olive oil as mold release when pressing wet PMC into it; can be bought ready-made or you can make your own with water, white glue, and shredded newsprint		
Plaster of Paris	Powdered gypsum	Readily available; moderately durable; resulting mold can be used repeatedly	Must be sealed (varnished) for use with metal clay; not the best for picking up fine detail; messy; requires mold release (with petroleum jelly, for example) when making the mold
	Comments: Requires a little olive oil as mold release when pressing wet PMC into it		

WORKING WITH LIVER OF SULFUR

There are many chemicals for adding patinas to metal surfaces. The one that I use, and suggest for use in the projects, is liver of sulfur (potassium sulfide). Liver of sulfur is a relatively safe chemical and, of the patina chemicals, it is the most innocuous. Because it generates fumes, however, you must make sure to work in an area that is actively ventilated. A solution of liver of sulfur produces a strong odor similar to that of boiled or rotten eggs. Wear rubber, latex, or nitrile gloves when handling it, or use nonreactive tweezers (stainless steel, bamboo, or plastic).

The liver of sulfur used in jewelry making is packaged in two different forms: as chunks or in solution. I recommend the chunks, which are packaged in an airtight, opaque container and retain their strength longer than the solution.

Preparing Chunk Liver of Sulfur

1. Break the chunk into small pieces. Wearing gloves or using tweezers, remove a piece of the liver of sulfur from its container and place it in two (doubled) heavy-duty plastic (freezer) bags. Place the bags on a steel anvil or bench block and, working with a mallet or hammer, reduce the size of the liver of sulfur to pieces smaller than a very small green pea. Because light and moisture will cause the chemical to deteriorate, slip these pieces into a small opaque, sealable container for storage until you are ready to use them (a black plastic film canister will do).

2. When you are ready to use the liver of sulfur, dissolve one of the small pieces in hot water in a small, nonreactive (stainless steel or Pyrex) bowl. Use the resulting solution immediately. The color of the solution should be a clear light yellow, lighter than the color of an egg yolk. A darker or more intense solution may produce a patina quickly, but can be fragile and flake off. You can store this solution for several days, after which it will have fully deteriorated. (Check with your municipal sewer department for specific information about the safe disposal of deteriorated liver of sulfur.)

Patinating the Fine Silver Bead

1. The bead should be polished and finished before the application of the patina. A brighter, more reflective surface on the metal will yield a more striking patina.

2. Before beginning the patination, clean and degrease the metal object by brushing vigorously with a soft-bristled brush (such as a toothbrush), hot water, and liquid dish-washing detergent. Then rinse it thoroughly.

3. Fine silver from metal clay that is to be patinated must be burnished, or it can retain some of the liver of sulfur solution and will therefore continue to darken. Burnishing may be done in one of several ways: by hand (with a steel jeweler's burnisher or by vigorously brushing with a jeweler's brass or steel brush and a few drops of liquid dishwashing detergent); in a rotary tumbler, using steel shot, water, and a few drops of liquid dishwashing detergent (for a minimum of 30 minutes to a maximum of 1 hour); or in a magnetic tumbler. I prefer this last method, because it's so convenient and fast.

4. After burnishing, rinse your bead in clean hot water, allowing the bead itself to become hot.

5. Drop the object in the hot liver of sulfur solution. Remove the object after a few seconds, either with gloved hands or tweezers, being careful not to scratch the object.

6. Rinse the bead in hot running water and reimmerse it in the solution. Repeat this immersion and rinsing procedure until the patina is as dark as you wish it to be. This process prevents an abrupt darkening of the metal and allows you some control over the patination process.

7. Rinse the bead in hot water with a little dishwashing liquid. You may also rinse with a few drops of soapy household ammonia in hot water, as this helps to neutralize the liver of sulfur. Remove the protective gloves.

Completing the Patina

First Method: To highlight and emphasize a textured surface, you will need a clean, 100 percent cotton cloth (old, clean white dress gloves are great for this purpose). Wrap your index finger in the cloth and dip it in oil (a light kitchen oil will work) and a little fine grade pumice (from jeweler's and woodworker's suppliers). Gently wipe your index finger across the surface of your object, removing the patina from the high spots and leaving the patina in the recesses. Wipe the surface with a clean section of the cloth. Rinse your piece in hot water and dishwashing liquid to remove the oil.

Second Method: To achieve an allover patina on the surface of your object, add a drop of liquid dishwashing detergent to the bristles of a brass jeweler's brush and lightly brush the surface of your object.

Creating a Colored Patina on Fine Silver

1. Follow the instructions above for preparing the liver of sulfur and patinating the fine silver bead, but rinse the bead in cold running water before reimmersing it in the patina solution. Cold rinsing will slow the patination and will prevent an abrupt darkening of the metal and allow you some control over the patination process.

2. The patina will go through a range of colors (from gold to brown to rose to violet to blue to black). You can work with this natural progression to create a metal object that glows with one or more of these colors. Adding a drop of household ammonia to the liver of sulfur will produce more vibrant roses and violets.

3. Continue immersing your object until it has the color you want.

4. Microcystalline wax (such as Renaissance Wax) is effective for coating the surface of a patinated piece so the piece retains its color. Be aware, however, that the wax will change the color hue and intensity somewhat.

Resources

In this section, I've listed some of the many suppliers of materials and tools for work with metal clay. I've also included contact information for organizations, guilds, schools, and art centers that will be helpful if you'd like to network and learn with others.

See the Further Reading section on pages 152–154 for a list of useful books and periodicals. On pages 154–156, you'll find contact information for the artists whose work appears in this book.

SUPPLIERS

Due to limited space, this is only an abbreviated list of suppliers. It includes suppliers that carry primarily metal clay products and also some suppliers of tools and equipment not specifically related to metal clay products.

Allcraft Tool and Supply
135 W 29th Street, Room 402,
New York, NY 10001
800.645.7124
Source for general jewelry-making supplies.

AMACO (American Art Clay Company)
6060 Guion Road,
Indianapolis, IN 46254-1222
800.374.1600
www.amaco.com
*Source for Friendly Plastic pellets
(thermo-plastic pellets for moldmaking).*

Art Clay World USA
4535 Southwest Highway,
Oak Lawn, IL 60453
866.381.0100
www.artclayworld.com
*Supplier of Art Clay products and equipment
(including: circle and other shape cutters) and
extruders; introductory and certification classes.*

Contenti
515 Narrangansett Park Drive,
Pawtucket, RI 02861
800.651.1887
www.contenti.com
*General jewelry making tools and equipment,
including a packaged set of tools for use with
metal clay.*

Cooltools
162 W Main Street, Suite M,
Whitewater, WI 53190
888.478.5060
www.cooltools.us
*Silk and Claymate lubricants and a wide range
of other metal clay tools, equipment, and
supplies, including the Ultralite kiln, circle and
other shape cutters, and extruders.*

Blick Art Materials
P.O. Box 1267, Galesburg, IL 61402
800.828.4548
www.dickblick.com
*General art supplies, Art Clay, Soft-Kut print-
ing blocks, linoleum cutters, shapers, waterbrushes, and circle and other shape cutters.*

Fire Mountain Gems and Beads
One Fire Mountain Way
Grants Pass, OR 97526
800.355.2137
www.firemountaingems.com
*Beads, findings, tools, Art Clay, and related
supplies.*

MED'A Creations
San Pablo, CA 94806
510.236.2313
mary@medacreations.com
www.medacreations.com
*Offers general classes and Precious Metal Clay
supplies, including circle and other shape cutters.*

Metal Clay Findings
49 Hurdis Street,
North Providence, RI 02904
888.999.6404
www.metalclayfindings.com
*Developer and supplier of fine silver findings for
use with metal clay.*

Metalliferous
34 West 46th Street, New York, NY 10036
212.944.0909
info@metalliferous.com
www.metalliferous.com
888.944.0909
Fax: 914.664.3778
*Jewelry-making materials and tools with a wide
range of textured metal sheets for clay texturing.*

Nasco
901 Janesville Avenue, PO Box 901,
Fort Atkinson, WI 53538
800.558.9595
www.enasco.com
*Safety-Kut block printing blocks; linoleum
cutters/carvers; supplies, tools, and equipment,
including Art Clay products, beveled clay cutters,
circle and other shape cutters, and waterbrushes.*

Otto Frei
126 2nd Street, PO Box 796,
Oakland, CA 94604
800.772.3456
info@ottofrei.com
www.ottofrei.com
General jewelry making tools and equipment, Art Clay products and tools, and Ultralite kiln.

PMC123.com
San Antonio, TX
210.656.8239
www.pmc123.com
Wide range of PMC products, including circle cutters and waterbrushes; general classes.

PMC Connection
8910 Mikuni Ave,
Northridge, CA 91324-3496
866.PMC.CLAY
www.pmcconnection.com
Precious Metal Clay products, including wood clay, shapers, and circle and other shape cutters; offers three levels of certification classes in metal clay; website presents extensive information useful when using metal clay.

PMC Supply.com
225 Cash Street, Jacksonville, TX 75766
800.388.2001
info@pmcsupply.com
www.pmcsupply.com
Source for Precious Metal Clay, kilns, and other silver clay tools and accessories; Evenheat PMC Kilns and metal clay kilns; tumblers, wood clay, Ultralite kiln, and shapers.

PMC Tool and Supply LLC
1 Feeder Street, Lambertville, NJ 08530
609.397.9550
www.pmctoolandsupply.com
General metal clay supplies, including Kaowool-insulated firing pad, shapers, and Ultralite kiln.

Reactive Metals
PO Box 890, Clarkdale, AZ 86324
800.876.3434
info@reactivemetals.com
www.reactivemetals.com
Good range of jewelry making tools and equipment, especially for reactive metals (titanium, niobium); supplier for sheets of Scotchbrite abrasive material.

Rio Grande
7500 Bluewater Rd,
Albuquerque, NM 87121
800.545.6566
www.riogrande.com
Extensive range of jewelry making materials, equipment, and tools, including a large selection of supplies and tools specifically for use with Precious Metal Clay (they were the first U.S. distributor of this material); offers substantial discounts through their Rio Rewards PMC Certification program.

Thompson Enamels
Mailing: PO Box 310 Newport, KY 41072
Order: 800.545.2776
www.thompsonenamel.com
Wide range of lead-free enamels and enameling tools and equipment.

Rings & Things
P.O. Box 450, Spokane, WA 99210
800.366.2156
www.rings-things.com
Range of Art Clay products and metal clay tools, including Kaowool firing pad.

Whole Lotta Whimsy
520.531.1966
staff@wholelottawhimsy.com
www.wholelottawhimsy.com
Wide range of metal clay (Art Clay and Precious Metal Clay), tools, and equipment, including circle and other shape cutters, shapers, waterbrushes, beveled cutters, and extruders; general classes.

ORGANIZATIONS AND GUILDS

PMC Guild
office@pmcguild.com
www.pmcguild.com
Features: Precious Metal Clay group; Fusion (newsletter); local chapters; discussion group; conferences; PMC Annual (exhibition book); biannual conferences; education.

Art Clay Society
4535 Southwest Highway,
Oak Lawn, IL 60453
866.381.0100
www.artclaysociety.com
Features: Art Clay group; local chapters; Newsletter; conferences; education.

Online Group
http://groups.yahoo.com/group/metalclay

EDUCATION
Online Information

PMC Connection
www.pmcconnection.com
Provides listing of both general and certification classes.

PMC Guild
office@pmcguild.com
www.pmcguild.com
Provides listing of both general metal clay and metal clay certification classes.

Society of North American Goldsmiths
www.snagmetalsmith.org/ProgramsResources/Educational_Institutions
Provides listing of jewelry and metal-related educational programs.

Craft Centers and Schools

This abbreviated list includes only some of the locations offering jewelry making workshops and classes, often including those in metal clay.

Many of the suppliers listed on pages 150–151 offer information on general metal clay classes and/or offer classes themselves.

Arrowmont School of Arts & Crafts
556 Parkway, PO Box 567,
Gatlinburg, TN 37738
865.436.5860
info@arrowmont.org
www.arrowmont.org

Brookfield Craft Center
286 Whisconier Road, PO Box 122,
Brookfield, CT 06804
203.775.4526
info@brookfieldcraftcenter.org
www.brookfieldcraftcenter.org

Haystack Mountain School of Crafts
PO Box 518, Deer Isle, ME 04627
207.348.2306
haystack@haystack-mtn.org
www.haystack-mtn.org

Mendocino Art Center
45200 Little Lake Street, PO Box 765,
Mendocino, CA 95460
800.653.3328
mendoart@mcn.org
www.mendocinoartcenter.org

Metalwerx
50 Guinan Street, Waltham, MA 02451
617.781.3854
www.metalwerx.com

Mid Cornwall School of Jewellery
Treesmill Farm, Tywardreath Par,
Cornwall, PL24 2TX, England
+44 (0) 1726 817 989
info@mcsj.co.uk
www.mcsj.co.uk

North Bennet Street School
39 North Bennet Street, Boston, MA 02113
617.227.0155
admissions@nbss.org; workshop@nbss.org:
www.nbss.org

Penland School of Crafts
PO Box 37, Penland, NC 28765
828.765.2359
office@penland.org
www.penland.org

Peters Valley Craft Center
19 Kuhn Road, Layton, NJ 0/851
973.946.5200
pv@warwick.net
www.petersvalley.org

Revere Academy of Jewelry Arts
760 Market Street, Suite 900,
San Francisco, CA 94102
415.391.4179
info@revereacademy.com
www.revereacademy.com/

Snow Farm: The New England Craft Program
5 Clary Road, Williamsburg, MA 01096
413.268.3101
info@snowfarm-art.org
www.snowfarm.org

Touchstone Center for Crafts
1049 Wharton Furnace Road
Farmington, PA 15437
800.721.0177
info@touchstonecrafts.com
www.touchstonecrafts.com

FURTHER READING

Here are some of the books and periodicals you might find useful as you pursue your work in metal clay. There are many more publications, more every day it seems, but these will help to answer many of the questions that you might have as you begin to explore metal clay, enameling, and jewelry making techniques.

Books

The Art of Enameling: Techniques, Projects, Inspiration
by Linda Darty
Lark Books

A recent addition to the many enameling books published; one of the best organized with information clearly presented and images that relate very well to the text.

The Colouring, Bronzing and Patination of Metals
by Richard Hughes
Watson-Guptill Publications

Explores the realm of metal coloring and patination; contains the most complete information on the subject.

Complete Metalsmith: ProPlus Edition
by Tim McCreight
Brynmorgen Press

Although there are many manuals that attempt to cover the field of making jewelry, this is one of the most concise and best organized for ease of use. Thos book is available in three formats: Student Edition, Professional Edition, and ProPlus Edition. I have selected the ProPlus Edition because it contains the Professional Edition, plus a CD that contains the full text of the book in a searchable and printable format and the text of two additional books (Practical Jewelry Rendering and Design Language).

Contemporary Enameling: Art and Technique
by Lilyan Bachrach
Schiffer Publishing

Individual artist's chapters focus on specific enameling methodology; richly illustrated with the work of many prominent enamellists.

Enameling on Metal Clay: Innovative Jewelry Projects
by Pam East
Kalmbach Publishing

Covers specifically vitreous enamels on metal clay; well written with clear instructions and useful information.

Enamelling on Precious Metals
by Jeanne Werge-Hartley
The Crowood Press

Good information and clear images, with a chapter devoted to Precious Metal Clay.

The Handbook of Metal Clay: Textures and Forms
by Hadar Jacobson
Textures Publishing

Collection of clearly illustrated and described projects that introduce a wide range of concepts, techniques, and tools, presented in an easy-to-use format.

Jewelry Concepts and Technology
by Oppi Untracht
Doubleday & Company

One of the most comprehensive volumes on jewelry making; a classic in the field with an enormous amount of information, but none on metal clay, because it was published before metal clay was available.

Keum-Boo on Silver; Techniques for Applying 24k Gold to Silver
by Celie Fago
Golden Hands Press

This self-published volume by one of the preeminent metal clay (and polymer) artists, clearly illustrates the process for applying 24k gold foil to the surface of a fine silver object, a technique particularly applicable to objects made using fine silver metal clay.

Making the Most of Your Flex-Shaft
by Karen Christians
MJAS/AJM Press

This book contains a thorough presentation of the many (and correct) ways of using a flex-shaft machine. If you own or are considering owning a flex-shaft, this book is indispensable.

Creative Metal Clay Jewelry: Techniques, Projects, and Inspiration and New Directions in Metal Clay: 25 Creative Jewelry Projects
by CeCe Wire
Lark Books

These are two of the best books for both beginning and advanced techniques—and everything in between. They contain good images and clear information and project instructions.

PMC Decade: The First Ten Years of Precious Metal Clay
by Tim McCreight
Brynmorgen Press

McCreight is the liaison with Mitsubishi and founder of the PMC Guild. This book celebrates the inspiring work created in metal clay and includes images of forty-seven artists' work, a critical essay by Donald Friedlich, a brief essay on the science behind PMC, and a thorough chronological history of Precious Metal Clay.

PMC Guild Annual
PMC Guild

This is the first edition of an annual juried showcase of excellent PMC work. Jeanette Landenwitch (Jury Chair and Director of the PMC Guild), Hadar Jacobson, Hattie Sanderson, and Robert Dancik, all accomplished metal clay artists, juried this edition.

PMC Technic: A Collection of Techniques for Precious Metal Clay
by Tim McCreight
Brynmorgen Press

This is a classy and thorough compilation of advanced techniques. Each chapter is dedicated to a specific technique and is written by individual metal clay artists.

Step-by-Step Bead Stringing: A Complete Illustrated Professional Approach
by Ruth F. Poris
Beadwork Books

This self-published book gives easy to understand beginning to advanced instructions for stringing beads. The instructions describe the use of simple tools and equipment, making it a good resource for beginners who are learning the basics of bead stringing.

Magazines and Periodicals

Art Jewelry
www.artjewelrymag.com

Monthly periodical for a wide range of jewelry making techniques, book reviews, instructional projects, features on jewelry artists and calendar of events; includes a section dedicated to instruction for beginning jewelry making techniques needed for the projects.

Craft Arts International
www.craftarts.com.au

Quarterly periodical presenting a wide range of international art/craft artists in an elegant format.

Lapidary Journal/Jewelry Artist

www.lapidaryjournal.com

Monthly periodical for a wide range of jewelry making techniques, book reviews, instructional projects, features on jewelry artists and calendar of events; includes listings of jewelry making classes and gem/jewelry shops.

Ornament

www.ornamentmagazine.com

This magazine, published five times a year, is the equivalent of having a jewelry/bead/wearable fiber gallery in your hands; offers feature articles on individual artists, jewelry making schools, ancient and modern beads, and exhibition and museum news.

ARTISTS' CONTACT INFORMATION

Maggie Bergman

email: info@maggiebergman.com.au
website: www.MaggieBergman.com.au

Maggie Bergman's work has been published in PMC Decade and in Art Jewelry and Australian Beader Magazine. Her work has been shown nationally and internationally, including in Revolution/Evolution, and she has taught metal clay since 2002. She brings her experience in drawing, sculpting, pottery, and printmaking to her jewelry making.

Gwen Bernecker

409 Rennard Drive
Exton, PA 19341
email: gwen@twoolivesstudio.com

Gwen Bernecker has a jewelry studio at her home in Chester County, Pennsylvania. She is certified in PMC and as an Art Clay instructor. She teaches nationally and is the founder of the Greater Philadelphia Metal Clay Guild. Her work has been published in extensively in periodicals and in PMC Decade.

Barbara Briggs

4860 Kopper Pond Road
Hanover, IL 61041
email: briggsdesigns@aol.com
website: www.BarbaraBriggsDesigns.com

Barbara Briggs has experimented with color, texture, and form by creating jewelry. She studied jewelry making at DeCordova Museum of Art and at College of DuPage and is certified in PMC.

Angela Baduel-Crispin

Bretagne, France
email: ange.est.la@wanadoo.fr
website: www.LAngeEstLa.com

Angela Baduel-Crispin is an award-winning Anglo-Brazilian artist who has been making jewelry since 1990 and has worked with PMC since 2003. Although initially self-taught, she has developed her skills through metalsmithing courses. She introduced PMC to France, where she lives, works, and teaches jewelry making.

Christopher C. Darway

529 Old Street Road
Feasterville, PA 19053
email: darwaydesign@earthlink.net

Chris Darway received a BFA in craft design from the Philadelphia College of Art and has been working in metals for over thirty years as a designer, teacher, and artisan. Over the years he has sold and exhibited work through galleries, shops, and craft shows nationally and internationally, including the ACC shows and Smithsonian Craft Show. He is currently a master lecturer in the crafts department at the University of the Arts in Philadelphia, the new president of the Pennsylvania Society of Goldsmiths, and one of the senior instructors for the Rio Rewards program.

Tonya Marie Davidson

2000 W Khaibar Place
Tucson, AZ 85704
email: tonya@wholetottawhimsy.com

Tonya Davidson is a senior instructor in PMC (since 2006) and a senior teacher for Art Clay (since 2002). She is a co-owner of Whole Lotta Whimsy, a company that develops and sells supplies and equipment for metal clay. She shown her work nationally and has had exposure in books and periodicals, including: PMC Decade and PMC Technic.

Catherine Davies-Paetz

cdp designs
3237 Chadbourne Road
Shaker Heights, OH 44120
PO Box 201512
Cleveland, OH 44120
phone: 216.491.1110
email: cdp@cdpdesigns.com
website: www.cdpdesigns.com

Catherine Davies-Paetz has been designing jewelry for more than thirty years, the last eight years of which she has been working extensively in metal clay. She is certified in PMC, teaches classes and workshops, and creates one-of-a-kind, custom designs and production jewelry in silver, 24k gold, enamel, beads, and pearls.

Marco Fleseri

1509 W. Rosemont
Chicago, IL 60660
email: marcofleseri@yahoo.com

Pat Gullett

119 Old Ridge Rd
New Milford, CT 06776
phone: 860.350.2663
email: ravenwoman3@gmail.com
website: www.howlingmoonstudio.com

Pat Gullett earned a BFA from the University of Illinois and an MA from Columbia College and has been a lifelong artist/instructor. Her jewelry and step-by-step projects have been published in Art Jewelry and PMC Studio. *Her work has been exhibited nationally and was selected as a 2007 NICHE Award Finalist.*

Hadar Jacobson
email: hadar@pacbell.net
Website: www.artinsilver.com
Hadar Jacobson is a self-taught jewelry artist and teacher who has practiced traditional jewelry fabrication for eighteen years and worked with metal clay for nine years. Her work has been published in professional magazines and shown in national exhibitions. She recently published The Metal Clay Handbook: Textures and Forms.

Nancy Karpel
PO Box 8691
New Haven, CT 06531
e-mail: karpelstudio@att.net
website: www.nancykarpeljewelry.com
Nancy Karpel has been a professional jewelry artist for over 32 years and began using PMC in 1997. Her work, which has won a NICHE Award and has been included in many publications, has been shown both nationally and internationally and is in the permanent collections of the White House and the National Air and Space Museum in Washington, DC

Terry Kovalcik
57 Pompton Road
Haledon, NJ 07508
email: VisualTwist@optonline.net
website: www.TerryKovalcik.com
Terry Kovalcik, a senior instructor in the Rio Rewards program, makes PMC jewelry under the company name Visual Twist. He strives to incorporate storytelling capabilities in ways that go beyond the simple ornamental nature of jewelry.

Jeanette M. Landenwitch
1921 Cliffview Lane
Florence, KY 41042
email: jmlandenwitch@yahoo.com
website: www.jmlcreations.com
Jeanette Landenwitch became the executive director of the PMC Guild in 2005 and has taught PMC, including certification classes, at numerous craft centers nationally. She has written many articles for periodicals in the field and is presently at work on a book on stonesetting with metal clay. Her work has been featured in exhibitions nationally and internationally, including in PMC Decade *(2007–2008) and* PMC Invitational Exhibition *(Japan, 2004–2005). She was the curator for the following exhibitions:* 57/1; Artists from the Premier Edition of the PMC Guild Annual *(2008); and* Revolution/Evolution: Contemporary Work in Precious Metal Clay *(2006).*

Wendy Wallin Malinow
10815 SW Southridge Drive
Portland, OR 97219-7860
email: eyefun@comcast.net
Wendy Wallin Malinow studied fine art and business at Lewis & Clark College in Portland, Oregon. She worked as an art director and illustrator through the eighties and continues to do illustrative work in the book and gift markets. Her polymer and PMC work has been shown in many exhibitions and shows nationally and internationally. Her work has been featured in many books, including PMC Decade, 400 Polymer Designs, 500 Pendants, 500 Necklaces, The Art of Jewelry: Polymer Clay, Metal Clay *and* Mixed Media Jewelry. *Wendy has won two first-place Saul Bell Design Awards and was a finalist for a third.*

Eleanor Moty
1441 North Day Road
Tucson, AZ 85715
email: ehmoty@wisc.edu
Eleanor Moty was one of the original fifteen metalsmith/artists participating in the Haystack Experimental PMC Workshop and she has presented numerous workshops on Precious Metal Clay. She is primarily recognized for her one-of-a-kind jewelry, which has been shown internationally, and for her pioneering research of photo-fabrication techniques. She is a professor emerita from the University of Wisconsin, Madison, having taught there for twenty-eight years.

Barbara Becker Simon
122 SW 46th Terrace
Cape Coral, FL 33914
website: www.bbsimon.com
Barbara Becker Simon earned a master of fine arts in metalwork and jewelry and is a senior instructor for Precious Metal Clay certification. She has taught internationally. Her work won second place (PMC) in the Saul Bell Design Award 2007 and has been published in Creative Metal Clay Jewlery: Techniques, Projects and Inspiration; New Directions in Metal Clay, *and in other books and major periodicals. Her work is in the collections of the Bead Museum (Washington, DC) and the Kobe Lampwork Glass Museum (Japan).*

Sabine Alienor Singery
email: contact@lesbijouxdalienor.com
website: www.lesbijouxdalienor.com
Sabine Alienor Singery has been creating crocheted wire jewelry and working with metal clay since 2006. She is a certified instructor of metal clay and the author of the first French-language book on metal clay, Bijoux Creatifs en Pâte d'argent *(Creative Jewelery in Silver Art Clay).*

Gordon Uyehara

email: gordon@honudream.com
website: www.honudream.com

Gordon Uyehara resides in Hawaii, where he is an artist/designer and an Art Clay silver senior instructor. Working with silver clay led him to small-scale design and wearable art. His piece, Ancient Life, was awarded second place (PMC) in the Saul Bell Design Award 2005. His motivation is to create pieces that are familiar and seductive while exploring the outer design limits of this relatively new art form. He is gradually incorporating traditional jewelry making techniques into his work as he learns them. His work has been shown in local, national, and international juried exhibitions.

Candice Wakumoto

PO Box 893113
Mililani, HI 96789
email: candicewakumoto@msn.com

Candice Wakumoto uses the medium of silver clay to create handcrafted works of art for personal adornment. Her work is inspired by the beauty of her home on Oahu, Hawaii. Her jewelry has received many awards in international and national competitions and has been featured in several books.

CeCe Wire

131 Fishback Avenue
Fort Collins, CO 80521
phone: 970.221.4115
cell: 970.690.6627
email: cecewire@frii.net

CeCe Wire is an artist and metalsmith with more than ten years of teaching experience in colleges and art centers, both nationally and internationally. She served as executive director of the PMC Guild for five years and has published two books on metal clay: Creative Metal Clay Jewelry: Techniques, Projects, Inspiration *and* New Directions in Metal Clay: 25 Creative Jewelry Projects. *Her work has been exhibited nationally and internationally.*

Jean Wydra

2520 Stern Drive South
Atlantic Beach, FL 32233
phone: 904.241.5604
email: rozbird@juno.com
website: www.rozbirdartjewels.com

Jean Wydra's art grows out of a passion for precious objects. Her focus has been the visual whole and how it stimulates the viewer's sense of rarity and preciousness. Her love of gemstones has permeated her work, resulting in an integration of stone and metal.

Acknowledgments

For the many years of our marriage, I have been inspired by and affirmed by my dear friend and spouse, Evan J. Soldinger. Now I have even more for which to thank him, because his clear project photography and images of my jewels enhance this volume. Grateful thanks go to my editor, Deborah Cannarella, whose faith in my ability to pull this off never flagged.

Mitsubishi, having embarked on the investigations that resulted in the development of Precious Metal Clay (PMC), provided the opportunity to expand my jewelry-making horizons and made this book almost inevitable. Thanks go also to Tim McCreight, for his continuing willingness to spread the word about PMC and to offer advice and answer questions, and to CeCe Wire for helping to answer many of my perplexing book-writing problems that surfaced (and there were a few).

I am especially grateful for the continuing inspiration of my students and the many metal clay artists who keep on sharing their experience with metal clay and its possibilities.

About the Author

Linda Kaye-Moses is an award-winning jewelry artist whose work and articles have appeared in *Lapidary Journal, Step-by-Step Jewelry, The Crafts Report, Metalsmith, Ornament, Art Jewelry, American Craft, American Style, the New York Times,* and *Craft Art International,* among others. Her work has also been featured in many one-person shows. Linda was the guest curator for the seminal Precious Metal Clay exhibition, *Milennial Metal,* held at the Lynn Tendler Bignell Gallery in Brookfield, Connecticut. She has also participated in numerous juried and invitational shows throughout the country and is a member of several professional organizations, including the PMC Guild, American Craft Council, and the Society of North American Goldsmiths. Linda lives in western Massachusetts with her husband, photographer Evan J. Soldinger.

Index